Wood Pellet Smoker And Grill For Beginners

The Ultimate Guide to a Perfect Barbecue with Recipes for BBQ and Smoked Meat, Game, Fish, Vegetables and More Like a Pro

Jordan West

© Copyright 2021 - All rights reserved.

TABLE OF CONTENTS

Introduction

YOu will obtain every secret to cooking with a Wood Pellet Smoker-Grill, and you will have tons of great recipes to try again and again. Plus, this can expect the same delicious flavors every single time. All you need to determine is to follow the ingredients and instructions strictly. You have many kinds of recipes, so you can try a new recipe every day and prove your cooking skills. Practicing will improve your understanding of obtaining great food every time and check your cooking techniques. Practicing will improve your ability to bring great flavors from this smoker-grill. To start cooking, go through the method of using your Wood Pellet Smoker-Grill and explaining the benefits, so you can leverage the equipment to its fullest ability when cooking. After that, you can pick your favorite recipes from the parts of poultry, red meat, pork, and seafood. Start by trying recipes from different categories. When you set a smoker to fair use and use the best kind of pellets, the flavor induced is so that not merely a guest who ends up eating the food but is sure to be amazed at the extraordinary culinary skills you possess.

Like ever, most recipes allow you to do a little makeshift. If you miss out on some get the best results, we prefer you to stick to the details as closely as possible. That means you will be working with different cooking methods, such as smoking, grilling, searing, and more. The instructions are trying various cooking methods, such as smoking, grilling, searing, and more. The instructions are smooth, so you are just working with different cooking methods, such as heat, grilling, searing, and more. The instructions are simple, so you need various smoking methods, grilling, burning, and more. The instructions are simple, so you just need to watch them as the videos had been presented. Here are some of the things we should keep in mind while getting the right Grill. Be careful of the size when deciding on the right barbecue grill. We must be mindful of the usage of the Grill because it will determine the extent of it. It can so happen one might want to throw a big party where they will need to have a big barbecue handy. On the other hand, someone might want to grill their veggies and proteins on a chilly winter evening on a more compact grill.

CHAPTER 1:

Why a Wood Pellet Smoked-Grill?

Hile very few people claim that the popularity of pellet Smoker and Grill stems from its increase of use and the outstanding marketing for this product, the majority of people agree upon the fact that Pellet Smoker and Grills are acquiring its unrivaled popularity thanks to the effectiveness of this product.

However, this new revolutionary appliance is still not known by many people; so, what is a Wood Pellet Smoker and Grill? So how can we use a Pellet Smoker and Grill?

What Is a Pellet Smoker and Grill?

To provide you with a clear answer about the Wood Pellet Smoker and Grill, let us start by defining this grilling appliance. In fact, Pellet Smoker and Grills can be defined as an electric outdoor Smoker and Grill that is only fueled by wood pellets. Wood Pellet is a type of fuel that is characterized by its capsule size and is praised for its ability to enhance more flavors and tastes to the chosen smoked meat. And what is unique and special about wood pellet as a fuel is that it can grill, smoke, roast, braise and even bake according is easy to follow instructions. I equipped with a control board that allows you to automatically maintain your desired temperature for several hours

Why Choose to Use a Wood Pellet Smoker and Grill?

The uniqueness of Pellet Smoker and Grills lies in the combination of the flavor and versatility it offers. Accurate, Pellet Smoker and Grills make an explosive mixture of sublime tastes and incredible deliciousness; it is a great Smoker and Grill appliance that you can use if you want to enjoy the taste of charcoal grill and at the same time you don't want to give up on the traditional taste of ovens. And what is more interesting about pellet Smoker and Grills is that, with a single button, you can grill, roast, bake, braise and smoke your favorite meat portions. Smoker and Grill and walk away; then, when you are back, you will be able to enjoy the great flavors you are craving. But how can we use a Pellet Smoker and Grill?

How to Use a Wood Pellet Smoker and Grill?

Pellet Smoker and Grills function based on advanced digital technology and many mechanical parts. The pellet Smoker and Grill are then lit while the temperature is usually programmed with the help of a digital control board. Pellet Smoker and Grills work by using an algorithm so that it allows calculating the exact number of pellets you should use to reach the perfect temperature. Every Wood Pellet Grill is equipped with a rotating auger that helps to automatically feed the fire right from the hopper to the fire to maintain the same temperature. And even as the food continues cooking, the wood pellet Smoker and Grill will continue to drop the exact number of pellets needed to keep the perfect cooking temperature. But what can we cook with a pellet Smoker and Grill?

CHAPTER 2:

History Of The Wood Pellet Smoked-Grill

PEllet grills originated from the olden pellet stoves. Although both pellet grills and pellet stoves run on wood pellets, there are some significant differences in the pellets that they burn. Besides hardwood, the pellets that are put into use for heating homes often consist of biomass scraps like bark and softwood. Both these things usually produce a terrible taste, and if they are ingested, they can be harmful.

This spearheaded a push toward all kinds of alternative heat sources, including, eventually, wood pellets. It is also relevant to note here that wood pellets came into existence in the late 1970s in the United States.

Regulates Cooking Temperature

When you use a wood fire pellet grill, you can rest assured that the heating within its chambers is even. So, your food will be cooked evenly from all sides. It also helps you control the temperature.

Hence, you get the perfect flavor in your food. Traditional grills do not offer this advantage because of their fluctuating temperature, which can be challenging to manage. Moreover, wood pellet grills offer the advantage of a heat diffuser plate on which you can place soaked hardwood chunks and wood chips. This further enhances the smoky effect of the food.

Offers Varied Cooking Options

The best thing about wood pellet smoker-grills is that they give you several options for easy cooking. They are versatile and let you quickly experiment with recipes and food. You can try various smoked recipes on the Grill and enjoy healthy cooking. The versatility of pellet grills is probably one of their best qualities. This ensures that you can enjoy several lip-smacking recipes in a matter of minutes. In addition, you can use pellet grills for cooking all kinds of food, from braised short ribs to chicken wings.

Offers Variety

Another significant advantage of using a wood pellet smoker-grill is that these smokers and grills come in a plethora of sizes and shapes. These grills are built and designed, keeping the preferences, needs, and tastes of customers in mind. Therefore, people who are looking for convenient cooking tools can always find something for themselves in wood pellet smokers and grills.

Cold Smoking

In addition to wood pellet fire grills and smokers, you can buy cold smokers from some companies. You can cook salmon and cheese dishes in these cold smokers.

Ease of Use

It is shared to see many people get intimidated by the idea of using a pellet grill. However, those fears are unfounded. While a pellet grill is quite different from your standard charcoal grills or gas grills, they are surprisingly easy to use. These grills come with controls that users can set and then simply forget about. They come with several features that make the entire process of grilling a piece of cake.

These grills usually do not require any lighter fluid, and they start with a single button. In addition, irrespective of the weather or the temperature outside, these grills can keep the temperature within a 10-degree range of your set temperature. This allows you to cook with zero effort like a pro. These grills are also designed to ensure that you do not overcook or over-smoke your food. Plus, they are never flare-up.

Value

While pellet smokers are slightly more expensive than standard grills, this is for a good reason. As mentioned above, these pieces of equipment offer the perfect combination of a smoker and a grill. They come with solid construction and stainless-steel components. This is precisely why they also come with an excellent four-year warranty.

This means that you will not buy these grills for summer only to dispose of them come winter. In addition, fuel efficiency is another one of their advantages. They come packed with double-wall insulation, which helps them sustain their temperatures better as well as use less fuel.

CHAPTER 3:

Shopping Guide For A Grill

How do Traeger Smokers work?

Raeger smokers use a very different heat generating system while sharing the 'set and forget' style of their gas and electric cousins.

Such cigarettes utilize cylindrical wooden cartridges, as the term suggests. A hopper on the side where you place the pellets is a standard setup.

Once you plug in the Grill and adjust the fire to a remote system, the pellets are moved and transformed into fire and smoke. The machine controls the temperature in your pellet cooker all over the pot.

There are some common kinds of grill controllers:

Three-position controls: generally, found on cheaper pellet cookers, these controls are set to three configurations, low (225 ° F), medium (325 ° F), and high (425 ° F). We are often referred to as LMH controls. During set intervals, they feed the pellets into the furnace, and you do not have a large amount of temperature power.

Multi-position controllers: these controls can be used in smaller increments to adjust the temperature. Pellets are fed in set loops that also do not give great precision to these controllers. In optimal settings, a multi-position controller usually is accurate + /-20 ° F. The inclusion of a Led panel is a useful function of these devices.

The non-PID device with one-touch: This form of control helps you to change the temperature in increments of 5-10 ° F. In fixed cycles, they still feed pellets, which means that they can solely deliver + /- 15-20 ° F accuracy. They also have LCD screens, one-touch controls, and many have meat sample inputs.

PID controllers: many found PID controllers to be the gold norm for grill controls. Temperatures are only a few degrees correct. Such a method of the device will also handle a programmable meat sample that operates along with the control mechanism to reduce the temperature until the meat is done. The pellet feed is continuously controlled to maintain the right temperature. They do have one-touch buttons and an LCD.

Durability and Construction Material

Don't be misled by an enticing pellet grill exterior. The maker may have made costs and used inexpensive parts to pick up on the interior even though there is plenty of stainless steel on the outside.

The most critical components of your Grill are the fire bowl, flame deflector, drop bowl, and grates. You have a cooker that lasts a lifetime because such parts are crafted from marine stainless steel.

If you are looking at a BBQ built from stainless steel, make sure it has a really good quality coating. As long as the paint blisters and chips continue to rust, the cooker deteriorates.

It can also be remembered that a pellet smoker made of high-quality materials is safer. High-quality materials preserve heat, allow more effective use of pellets, and help sustain the temperature during cold weather.

Size of the Hopper

Your pellet cooker's hopper is the tub that houses the pellets ready to go into the furnace. The scale of your hopper thus ultimately determines the length of your cooks. Therefore, it proves irritating to settle for a hopper that's too low, as your cooks won't be distant.

As a guide, you will find a pellet grill with a 40-pound hopper at the standard smoking temperatures for about 40 hours. In view of the fact that some cooks take about 20 hours, for example, an 18-pound hopper will be problematic.

And remember, your cooker will use even more fuel to raise the smoker and maintain temperature when you live in a colder climate.

You can buy hopper extensions for your grill pellet. Make sure that the hopper extender you are purchasing is compatible with your pellet smoker and the supplier is healthy.

Plan how much cooking real estate you need

You have to ask yourself a few questions before you know how big your cooker needs to be. How many people am I going to cook for? Do I plan to cook huge cuts or even a whole pig?

Remember, bigger doesn't mean better always. A large pellet cooker can only mean wasted pellets.

An unusual characteristic of pellet smokers is that the cooking region is also dry. As a rule, there should be no variation in temperature between the top rack and the bottom rack during cooking.

Despite this, let us think about the disparity between the primary cooking area and the total cooking region. The central cooking field applies to the field on the central pot. The overall cooking area takes secondary racks into account.

A broad cooker with a primary cooking area of 500 square inches may therefore be of less benefit to you than a cooker with a limited cooking area, which includes a primary 450 square inch rack and a secondary 125 square inch rack when you cannot be bothered to do arithmetic, 575 square centimeters of the total area for cooking.

The bottom line is – make an inventory of what you need and don't presume that it's cheaper.

Common features and Capabilities

In comparison to the typical charcoal or offset smokers, a whole lot of bells and whistles may be used with pellet grills.

WIFI: companies are beginning to benefit from the fact that pellet smokers have a designed computer inside them. By integrating Wi-Fi, the temperature of your Grill can be monitored and controlled from almost anywhere, as long as there is the internet. Companies such as Green Mountain Grills also provide free software that you can access and use for supreme convenience.

Meat samples: Some pellet cookers have controlled outputs to allow meat samples to be plugged in directly. You can then see readings taken from your meat easily on your cooker's computer.

Grilling options: Pellet cookers have a downside in the past because of their lack of grilling capabilities. Some manufacturers have made it possible to grill either by removing part of the diffuser plate or by supplying a special grilling area in the cooker.

Add-ons: Manufacturers often offer a range of supplements. Check for the standard features and what add-ons are at a surcharge. Some add-ons are offered independently from the manufacturer by companies. If your particular cooker has an essential feature but is not a standard feature, make sure it is available as an add-on before you buy the cooker.

Length of Warranty

In pellet smokers, there are some relatively high-tech components. Moving parts are also available, such as the hammer. This means that your cooker may break down, and you may not be able to fix it. Make sure you understand exactly how your warranty is extended, what it will cover, what it is void, and where your smoker will need to get in for any reparations.

Warranties vary among manufacturers, so do not be afraid to ask many questions.

Pellet Consumption

No one loves a pellet dog, a pellet burner that chews needless pellets.

If your pellet cooker is too thin, the cooker's body loses heat. It uses a lot of pellets to keep the temperature.

You will also use many pellets if the metal is too thick. The walls of a thick smoker act as a 'heat sink.' Heat is removed from the stove and stored in the cooker's walls. So, it takes a lot of pellets to reach the desired temperature in the cooking area. Although thick walls are desirable for certain types of cookers, in pellet smokers, they are not required.

Research and discover how many pellets the smoker burn per hour. Everything up to one pound an hour is OK at smoking temperatures. Bruce Bjorkman of MAK, for example, claims that his barbecues only use about 1/2 pound an hour for the smoke.

Beware of Gimmicks

There is a thin distinction between the practical inventions and gimmicks in the field of pellet smokers. Companies want to stand out above the rest because of increasing competition between manufacturers.

That's not to say all the features are just gimmicks and should be rejected as such. In the end, you have to worry about whether the pellet smoker apps are of particular value to you.

If the feature is something that you'd consider helpful, is it included at the expense of other, more important things like pellet use or durability?

However, if you live in a cold climate, and it freezes outdoors, being able to control your cook from inside your warm home may be an appealing feature. If that's the case, then Davy Crockett of Green Mountain Grills might be your ally right up there.

Customer Service

As expected, Awesome Ribs has excellent customer service value advice, particularly for pellet grills.

A dedicated customer service team will likely exist by buying from a more significant, established company. It also means that if you need their help, the company will probably be down the path for around a few years.

A smaller business will provide more intimate and consistent support on the flipside, and your pellet grill concept really would be familiar to the people you approach

You won't figure out if the company fits in when it comes to consumer care until you pose queries and provide straightforward answers.

Price

Pellet grills vary considerably in size. Others will save you several hundred dollars, and some will cost you thousands of dollars. A word of advice-do does not compare a cheap cooker with a good cooker for results.

A cheap cooker will save you early on, but if it continues to rust, after a few short years, you do not get a good warranty, and the customer service does not match, you may spend more cash in the long run.

On the other hand, if you bought all of the bells and whistles but didn't use them, you'll have wasted your hard-earned cash when a cooker that costs less would probably have done the trick.

Please check any of the above information before acquiring a currency. See what you can do with your profession, and ask certain questions. Then, what you must do is love your fresh cooker!

Given the wide price range, it's important to decide if you want to buy a pellet smoker. Going through a guide is definitely an ideal way of ensuring you have not forgotten anything.

The Pros and Cons of Purchasing a Smoker with a Pellet

Because of its convenience and versatility, most people choose a pellet-style smoker. Just like a cigarette, you offer:

Set it down and forget it, just make sure that the hopper is full of pellets and set your desired temperature, and you don't have to worry about that much else.

Easy temperature regulation – Some pellet smokers require you to dial up to five degrees at temperature, and the device is doing an outstanding job of holding the temperature constant.

There are also a few advantages distinctive to cooking with a pellet smoker:

Ultra-effective fuel – Pellet smokers with a super-powerful convection fan are close to your home oven, but you waste much less on pellet than on oil.

Less energy washing – any time you barbecue, charcoal smokers will create a little mess. You would need to clear the fireplace now and again with a pellet grill, but it is uncommon (think about per 60 uses).

CHAPTER 4:

Mastering Your Grill

THe Grill is the cooking system in which the food rests on bars of different shapes and sizes, and, under these, the fuel in the form of firewood or coal heats at the same time the iron and the food that, little by little, is cooking.

An important aspect to consider when choosing a grill is the type of bar that can be round, in V, or square.

The round bar is the most generous with the product since when falling on the embers, the fat of the product that we are cooking generates a cloud of smoke that aromatizes it. This can indeed raise the flame, but if we know how to handle it, the result is superior from the gastronomic point of view.

The V-bar, on the other hand, is easier to handle since it picks up the fat that releases the food to a grease trap, and it is more difficult for flames to be generated, but instead, we lose in aromas. It is a system that is widely used in hospitality since it allows cooking more quickly and without problems, but it does not make much sense for a domestic grill.

Also, the square bar is similar from the gastronomic point of view to the round. It is very popular in the United States, but in Europe, it is difficult to find it.

Apart from the type of bar, which can be chosen in most models, there are fixed, semi-fixed, and portable grills.

If we have a large garden, we may be interested in installing a working grill, which can be found in different sizes from 100 euros (although a good one, for 5 or 6 people, does not fall below 300). These are modeling whose installation is more complex, but they are a good option in country houses where there is adequate space to install it. However, these are less versatile instruments and whose purchase is made almost as a function of the available space.

The semi-fixed grills are prefabricated structures designed to cram in a reserved space for these. They usually also have a drawer to collect the ashes. It is a good option if there is adequate space to install it and we do not want to get involved with a grille, much more expensive.

The Barbecue

The barbecue is simply a grill with a lid, an additive that at first glance may not be decisive, but that makes the invention a much more complex kitchen system because, if it is lowered, it transforms it into an oven that cooks food from the controlled form. Also, thanks to the lid, the barbecue serves to smoke food, both cold and hot and makes the instrument much safer because if you have to leave the fire for any reason, just lower this and close the shot to stay calm.

The barbecue is, in fact, a relatively recent invention. In 1950, George Stephen, known as the Newton of the barbecues, had a party to inaugurate his new house, he did not know how to control the fire of his work grill, and the food was scorched. That was when he thought about creating an improved grill.

There is nothing like cooking open flame food. The techniques are simple, cleaning is easy, and grilled food tastes amazing.

CHAPTER 5:

The Fundamentals Of Wood Pellet Grilling And Smoking First Time

Ith the hundreds of different varieties and brands of wood pellets, it is often difficult to identify which brand to consider. If you are not sure what brand to opt for, it might help to try at least the top three brands you know of and compare their efficiency.

Appearance

The first factor to consider when choosing a brand of wood pellets is the appearance of the pellets. After using wood pellets for some time, you will be able to tell and judge their quality simply by how they appear.. Brands adhere to certain standards, so this is not a concern. Nevertheless, you need to understand that when it comes to pellet fuels, length matters, as it will affect the performance of the pellets. The dust you will find in the packaging is also another to consider. It is normal to see fines once you open the bag, but if there are an unusual number of fines, it means the pellets aren't of good quality.

Texture

The texture of the pellets is another thing. Wood pellets have a certain texture in them. If you feel that the pellets are smooth and shiny, it means they are of good quality. The same is true if the pellets do not have cracks. If the pellets are too rough with unusual racks on the surface, it means the pellets are bad. This is usually a result of incorrect pressing ratio and moisture content of the raw materials used in making the pellets.

Smell

Wood pellets are made by exposing them to high temperatures within a sealed space. During the process, the lignin contained in the biomass material is mixed with other elements, producing a smell of burnt fresh wood. If the pellets smell bad, there is a huge chance they have not been processed properly or contain impure, raw material.

Aside from the appearance, texture, and smell of the wood pellets, another way to check their quality is to see how they react with water. Put a handful of pellets in a bowl of water and allow them to settle for several minutes. If the pellets dissolve in the water and expand quickly, this means they are of good quality. On the other hand, if the pellets do not dissolve within minutes but instead expand and become hard, it means they are of bad quality.

Finally, try burning some of the pellets, as well. If the wood pellets are of excellent quality, the flame they produce will be bright and brown. If the flame they produce, on the other hand, is dark in color, it means the quality of the pellets is not good. Also, good-quality pellets produce a little ash, so if the pellets leave you with a lot of residues, it is a sign that the pellets are bad.

Right Wood For Right Meat, Right Temperature

Choose the type of meat that tastes good with a smoky flavor. Following meat goes well for Smoking.

Beef: ribs, brisket, and corned beef.

Pork: spareribs, roast, shoulder, and ham.

Poultry: whole chicken, a whole turkey, and big game hens.

Seafood: Salmon, scallops, trout, and lobster.

With so many recipes to try with your pellet grill, it is easy to get overwhelmed right away. Follow this useful guide below to know the temperature and time it requires to get the perfectly flavored meat each time.

- Beef briskets are best cooked at 250 degrees using the smoke setting for at least 4 hours by itself and covered with foil for another 4 hours.

- Pork ribs should be cooked at 275 degrees on the smoke setting for 3 hours and covered with foil for another 2-3 hours.

- Steaks require 400-450 degrees for about 10 minutes on each side.

- Turkey can be cooked at 375 degrees for 20 minutes per pound of meat. For smoked turkey, the heat settings should be around 180-225 degrees for 10-12 hours or until the inside of the turkey reaches 165 degrees.

- Chicken breasts can be cooked at 400-450 degrees for 15 minutes on each side.

- A whole chicken cooks at 400-450 degrees for 1.5 hours or until the internal temperature reaches 165 degrees.

- Bacon and sausage can be cooked at 425 degrees for 5-8 minutes on each side.

- Hamburgers should be cooked at 350 degrees for at least 8 minutes for each side.

- You can smoke salmon for 1-1.5 hours and finish with a high setting for 2-3 minutes on each side.

- Shrimps cook at 400-450 degrees for 3-5 minutes on each side. If you prefer a smokier flavor, set the temperature at 225 degrees for about 30 minutes.

Difference Between Hot And Cold Smoking

Cold Smoking

Usually, the Smokehouse temperature for cold Smoking is around 68-86 degrees F. In this process, the food is not cooked or smoked, cold Smoking only provides a Smokey flavor to it, and still, the meat and vegetables remain moist. This technique is mostly a flavor enhancer for the food, which is, later, going to be roasted, baked, or cooked in any other process rather than Smoking.

To cold-smoke meat like a pro, you will need to measure preservatives and salt correctly, set the temperature of the smoker rightly, measure the internal temperature of the meat with a high-quality thermometer, clean and maintain the chamber of the smoker properly and finally safely store meat to avoid bacteria growth (sodium nitrate can help to prevent bacteria growth).

Hot Smoking

In hot Smoking, we use a combination of heat and smoke for cooking food and getting it served immediately. Most food cooked by this method is marinated for hours before being cooked. Hence, there is no need for curing since the meat/food is prepared and served immediately.

Hot Smoking occurs between the temperatures of 126-176 degrees F. In this temperature, the food is thoroughly cooked, moist, and very flavorful. In hot Smoking, it is not preferred to smoke the food at more than 186 degrees F because doing so will make the food shrink excessively, lose all its moisture and fat content, and reduces the yield. The time required for Smoking varies depending on the type of food that is being hot smoked. When carrying out hot Smoking, there is a need to pay attention to the internal temperature of the food.

Basic Preparations

Getting Meat Ready

Prepare meat according to the recipe. Sometimes meat is cured, marinated, or simply seasoned with the rub. These preparation methods ensure smoked meat turns out flavorful, tender, and extremely juicy.

Brine is a solution to treating poultry, pork, or ham. It involves dissolving brine ingredients in water poured into a huge container, and then adding meat to it. Then let soak for at least 8 hours and after that, rinse it well and pat dry before you begin smoking.

Marinate treat beef or briskets and add flavors to it. It's better to make deep cuts in meat to let marinate ingredients deep into it. Drain meat or smoke it straightaway.

Rubs are commonly used to treat beef, poultry, or ribs. They are a combination of salt and many spices, rubbed generously all over the meat. Then the meat is left to rest for at least 2 hours or more before smoking it.

Before smoking meat, make sure it is at room temperature. This certifies the meat is cooked evenly and reaches its internal temperature at the end of the smoking time.

Grilling Tips

So, now let us focus on some of the best tips and tricks you can use to become a smart chef and ace the art of using the wood pellet grill.

- Never ignore the use of upper racks. If you can place a water pan beneath the rack, it will allow for even better cooking.

- Always make it a point to choose the right pellets when using the Grill. If you want to have a specific flavor, use flavored wood pellets. You also have mixed variants. Mostly, the food-grade version is a recommended choice.

- When the 40-pound bag of pellet is gone, make sure to thoroughly clean the Grill.

CHAPTER 6:

Start-up Process

THe Grill is designed to be easy to operate and use. After purchasing a Traeger Wood Pellet Grill & Smoker, the first step is to assemble the cooking appliance. Instructions for the assemble will be present in the accompanying Owner's Manual. Once assembled, acquaint yourself with some of the components itemized above.

Here is a quick step-by-step instruction on how to start a fire in the Wood Pellet Grill:

Open the Steel Door and remove the following components from the Grill: porcelain grill grate, the heat baffle, and grease drain pan.

Ensure the Grill Switch is in the "O" position (OFF).

Switch ON the Grill ("|" position) and turn the thermostat controller to Smoke. Check if the Auger is rotating. You will be able to notice the rotation of the Auger through the pellet hopper. Also, place your hand over the Firepot to feel the movement of the convection blower. The Hot Rod should start to turn red.

Fill the hopper with specially designed Traeger Barbecue Pellets and turn the thermostat controller to High.

Switch the thermostat controller to Smoke and allow the wood pellet flames in the Firepot to rise. Then, switch the thermostat controller to the Shutdown cycle to cool down the Grill.

Reset the components (porcelain grill grate, the heat baffle, and grease drain pan) of the Grill to their proper position. Line the drain pan with heavy-duty aluminum foil for easy cleaning.

Always preheat Grill at the desired temperature for 10 minutes before placing food on the grates.

CHAPTER 7:

Maintenance

Wood pellet grills are incredibly convenient. But it is important to keep in mind that you are still playing with live fire. You'll want to be prepared to deal with accidents and other issues. Each pellet grill smoker's owner's manual has official information on safety, troubleshooting, and maintenance.

If you are a new wood pellet grill owner, the first step in safety is to follow the manufacturer's instructions for the initial firing of the Grill. This will burn off any manufacturing oils and bits of Styrofoam packaging that may remain on cooking surfaces.

Never use your wood pellet grill in an enclosed area. Dangerous gasses can accumulate quickly. Grilling inside your home is obviously a smoky and bad idea, but also do not grill in enclosed porches and tents, which are less obviously dangerous.

To stay safe (and be able to enjoy your delicious smoker results), keep the following safety tips in mind at all times.

Safety 101

Have a dedicated fire extinguisher for your grill area (and another for your kitchen).

Never attempt to move a hot grill.

Follow the manufacturer's standard starting, preheating, and shutdown procedures. These steps will allow you to safely prime and ignite and later extinguish and clear your auger and firepot. The procedures help prevent the unsafe accumulation of pellets in the firepot.

The Grill will produce airborne hot embers, so keep kids, pets, flammable liquids, and vinyl siding a safe distance away from it for the entire cooking process.

Don't smoke with strange wood, particularly pellets that were not produced specifically for cooking. Non–food-safe pellets can be comprised of scrap wood. Construction scrap wood is often treated with toxic chemicals and other undesirable finishes that you wouldn't want to ingest.

Wood pellet grill smoker manufacturers don't want you to leave these cookers on for hours fully unattended. They express this in the owner's manual fine print. You'll also notice that in sales photos, they play it safe—the cook is always in eyeshot across the yard, relaxing in a chaise, or in the kitchen, keeping the cooker in the view from the window.

Never operate your wood pellet grill in the rain. Remember, your Grill relies on electricity to operate, and electric machines should never get wet. Plus, wood pellets are sensitive to moisture and will swell, disintegrate, and make a mess when wet.

Unplug your wood pellet grill when not in use, and avoid linking long extension cords. Even though the Grill generates its heat with burning wood, you still have possible electricity dangers. Remember, too, that your pellet grill won't operate if you lose power.

Accidents and mistakes occur all the time, but rest assured that your wood pellet grill is constructed with safety in mind and is safer to operate than charcoal and stick-burning smokers. This is because you don't have to add wood too hot coals to stoke the fire manually. With a wood pellet grill, the small firepot is tucked away inside the Grill and stoked thanks to the auger and the thermostat automatically.

Troubleshooting Tips

Be sure always to use your manufacturer's start-up and shutdown procedures. These critical steps ensure that your auger and firepot do not accumulate fuel.

If you feel like your Grill is struggling to maintain heat, cold temperatures may be the culprit. Your wood pellet grill's thermostat should compensate and have your auger and firepot work harder. Windy conditions can be a sneaker problem. When possible, position your Grill to avoid the direct wind. Specially constructed insulated grill covers are available from manufacturers (like Traeger) to combat exceptionally windy and cold conditions. It may seem odd for a grill to wear a sweater, but the fireproof material can safely provide needed insulation in windy and extra-cold conditions.

Any smoker is susceptible to delayed cook times due to prying eyes. Every time you open the cook chamber to peek, it can add take up to 15 minutes to regain temperatures. A right wood pellet grill's thermostat can combat this better than most other types of smokers, but if you think your cook times are longer than they should be, it's worth evaluating. As the saying goes, "If you're looking', you aren't cooking'."

Occasional ash cleanup is necessary to keep your Grill in profitable operation. Be sure to do your cleaning before the procedure, or at least 12 hours after any ignition.

A dependable power source is essential. Unlike charcoal and gas grills, wood pellet grills require electricity to stoke wood pellets into the firepot. A blown fuse or any interruption in power will make your Grill inoperable.

Maintenance Tips

Keep it clean. Your wood pellet grill requires little maintenance other than an occasional removal of ash from the firepot. When fully cool, you can use a shop vac to remove excess ash in and around the firepot and cook chamber. This is recommended after three to five cooks (or after exceptionally long cooks).

Vacuum the areas in and around the hopper occasionally, as they can accumulate sawdust and pellet remnants after use.

Clean your grill grate after each use. Porcelain-coated grates should be scrubbed with a nonmetallic brush to protect the porcelain finish.

Never use sprays or liquids to clean the interior of your wood pellet grill.

Use a cover when the Grill is not used to protect from bleaching sunlight, moisture, and nesting insects.

If you are having ignition or temperature problems, visually inspect the firepot. Over time, the firepot is the most commonly replaced part on wood pellet grills; due to intense heat and constant use, it is more susceptible to corrosion and wear. You can replace yours with any preferred stainless-steel firepots.

CHAPTER 8:

How To Clean Your Trigger Grill?

IT is very important to know how to correctly maintain and clean your Traeger grill. You made the great choice of buying a grill that will last a lifetime, so why don't ensure that it runs smoothly for years?

To care for your Traeger grills, you have to know its main components. You are most likely to call a repair service, if you have a problem, you still need to know how your Grill is built, even just for cleaning it properly.

There are eight main components of the machine which work together to provide you with results that you won't have with any other grill.

The main components are listed below:

Hardwood Pallets

These are the most important part of the Grill. They function as the main fuel for the Grill to work. All-natural hardwood flavorings can seep into your food while cooking through them. You can put any type of wood you want to bring a distinct taste to your dish.

Hopper

The flavoring happens here as the wood ignites and cooks the food. 100% wood with no charcoal or gas connection required.

Controller

The knob enables you to set the temperature of your choice and regulate it during the cooking process.

Induction Fan

The fan turns on as you turn on the grill and heat the food evenly using the convection process for cooking. The Fan transfers hot air to the entirety of the Grill, making it evenly distributed.

Auger

It is a screw-like device that picks and places the wood pellets into the firepot to start the ignition process.

Hot Rod

This is where the pellets meet the fire and fire catches on. It is at the end of the auger.

Firepot

Automatically fire is turned on, which ignites the hotrod and causes pellets to catch fire.

Drip Tray

This piece of metal just above the fire prevents it from directly reaching the Grill and reduces charring on food. It allows heat and smoke to pass through.

Ensuring your Grill is clean and free of built-up grease and debris is critical for keeping the pure, wood-fired flavor of your Grill intact. The best way to ensure this is through regular cleanings and maintenance of your Grill.

NOTE: Make sure that your Grill is switched off and not connected to the electrical outlet!

You'll want the following items on hand:

• Wooden Grill Grate Scrape

• Grease Cleaner. Trager markets a Traeger All-Natural Grease Cleaner, but your normal kitchen grease cleaner will work just as well. Even better, if you clean it frequently, you might want to consider using vinegar or lemon juice diluted with water (at 60%) in a spray bottle.

• Drip Tray Liners

• Bucket Liners

• Shop Vac

• Paper Towels

• Bottle Brush

• Disposable Gloves

Step 1 Spray grates with the grease cleaner

Step 2 Spray inside of the chimney

Step 3 Remove and clean grates with the Wooden Grill Grate Scrape. Don't use wire brushes and wipe the grates down with a cleaning cloth or heavy-duty paper towels for this.

Step 4 Remove drip tray liner

Step 5 Remove the drip tray

Step 6 Remove heat baffle

Step 7 Vacuum inside of the Grill.

Step 8 Scrub inside of the chimney with a bottle brush. Again, don't use wire brushes and wipe the grates down with a cleaning cloth or heavy-duty paper towels for this.

Step 9 Spray walls with your grease cleaner

Step 10 Let soak and wipe down with paper towels

Step 11 Reinsert heat baffle

Step 12 Reinsert drip tray

Step 13 Insert new drip tray liner

Step 14 Insert new bucket liner

Step 15 Reinsert grates

You don't have to go through the process every time you Grill; after all, the meat also takes its flavor from the charred and impregnated grates from all the previous barbecues. But you should do it twice, or three times per grilling season, if you use it frequently. If you are cooking something particularly greasy, we would recommend that you clean it right after. It will make the job a lot easier if you don't let the fat congeal.

To avoid problems and making the cleaning process a bit easier, here are some helpful tips for routine maintenance:

Invest in a cover. The Traeger covers are a bit expensive but aesthetically pleasing. If you don't want to buy a Trager cover, then make sure to cover it carefully with a plastic sheet. If your Traeger grill is stored outside during wet weather, you risk that water gets into the hopper. When the pellets get wet, they expand and may clog your auger. Also, you cannot cook with wet wood.

Change the foil on your grease pan often, and clean underneath the foil as well.

Empty the grease bucket. Yuck, I know! But it is a simple enough job: empty the grease in something you can discard, such as a plastic bottle; don't pour it down the drain or in the gutter! Clean the bucket with hot water and soap or, to make your job easier, line the bucket with aluminum foil that you can simply discard.

Wipe down the exterior surfaces. The Trager grills are beautiful objects, so keep the powder coating looking new! Use warm water and soap and wipe it with a clean cloth or paper towels. Don't use abrasive cleaners or scouring pads!

CHAPTER 9:

How To Clear An Auger Jam

Pellet grill is essentially a multi-functional grill designed so that the compressed wood pellets end up being the real fuel source. They are outdoor cookers and tend to combine smokers' different striking elements, gas grills, ovens, and even charcoal. The very reason which has cemented their popularity for ages have to be the kind of quality and flavor that they tend to infuse in the food you make on them.

Not only this, by varying the kind of wood pellet you are using, but you can also bring in the variation in the actual flavor of the food as well. Often, the best chefs use a mix and match technique of wood pellets to infuse the food with their signature flavor that have people hooked to their cooking in no time.

A wood pellet smoker grill's clinical definition is smoking, grilling, roasting, and baking barbecue using compressed hardwood sawdust such as apple, cherry, hickory, maple, mesquite, oak, and other wood pellets. It is a pit. Wood pellet smoker grills provide the flavor profile and moisture that only hardwood dishes can achieve. Depending on the manufacturer and model, the grill temperature on many models can be well over 150 ° F to 600 ° F. Gone are the days when people say they cannot bake on wood pellet smoking grills!

Wood pellet smoker grills offer the succulence, convenience, and safety not found in charcoal or gas grills. The smoke here is not as thick as other smokers familiar to you. Its design provides the versatility and benefits of a convection oven. A wood pellet smoker grill is safe and easy to operate.

The auger aims to ensure that the pellets get pushed down to the fire pot at the pre-configured speed, determined by the yard control panel showing the temperature. As soon as the shots reach the fire pot, an ignition rod creates a flame that causes smoke production.

Also, a fan is present at the bottom, which helps push both the generated heat and smoke upwards on the Grill and allows for the convection style of even cooking.

That happens to be the primary mechanism of the working of a wood pellet grill. Knowing the different parts of the wood pellet grill and the working tool will prepare you better to ensure that you can use the Grill correctly.

However, before we venture further into the recipes, we will focus on some essential points about these grills. That is because the right knowledge is crucial to ensuring that you know what you are getting into.

CHAPTER 10:

Maintaining Temperature

For you to achieve the perfect temperature, you've got to be able to control your Grill. The wood pellet smoker grill lets you do just that, with the controller, which adjusts both the flow of pellets and air, so that the temperature you've chosen remains constant. You should keep in mind that some manufacturers create their controllers, while others enlist a third party's services. Either way, it helps to be able to tell which controller is which. You want the kind that makes it possible to precisely set and control the temperature of your wood pellet smoker grill. You'll find that there are three kinds of controllers:

Analog Controllers. These are your standard units. They'll typically give you exactly three temperature set points: Low, medium, and high, also known as LMH. The entry-level wood pellet smoker grills are the ones that come with this sort of controller. You're not likely to find a thermocouple temperature probe or an RTD that could give the feedback loop.

I shouldn't have to point out that analog controllers are far from the best sort. The temperature fluctuates a lot when you use them, and it doesn't self-correct when it comes to ambient temperatures. All you can do is set the timer for turning the auger on and off for the low, medium, and high temperatures, which the manufacturer already preset. Could there be a better option?

Digital Controllers. These controllers are better than the analog controllers in that they have an RTD temperature probe, which gives you that much-needed feedback loop for flawless cooking. You'll find that most of the digital controllers out there have an increment setting of 25 degrees Fahrenheit. Once you've got the RTD temperature probe installed, you can have an even better substitute for the analog, LMH controllers. It pretty much works like your standard home thermostat.

All you have to do is enter your preset temperature, and once that is reached, the controller will switch the auger on for a set number of seconds, then off again for a set number of seconds. It idles for a bit, unless the temperature deviates from your preset number. Once that happens, the cycle repeats itself. Some digital controllers will let you set up how long you want your unit to idle. That way, ambient temperatures are accounted for.

Proportional Integral Derivative Controllers. Also known as PID controllers, these bad boys are the best value for your money. They are more advanced than the analog and digital controllers, which means even better temperature control. They have a thermocouple temperature probe with a control loop feedback, which helps check the temperature you want against the current temperature consistently; then it makes the required adjustments.

With a PID controller, you have the option of setting the cooking temperature in increments of 5 degrees. The auger feed rate can also be adjusted using the controller. There will be a variable number of fan speed settings, which help greatly keep the temperature stable, always keeping it within no more than 5 degrees Fahrenheit of the temperature you've set. This means that it doesn't get better than the PID controller when it comes to controlling temperature.

You'll find that the best wood pellet smoker grills have a PID controller already installed, and run by the most sophisticated programming to give you the precision you need. There are even control systems with two or more meat temperature probes, and have even more settings that give you the flexibility you need for cooking.

All that said, the absolute least you should settle for when it comes to getting a wood pellet smoker grill is the kind with a digital controller. If you can get a PID controller, that would be even better.

CHAPTER 11:

Choosing The Right Pellets

MArk - The pellet grill has only been around for about 30 years and has only attracted public attention for 10 to 15 years. As such, there are only a relative handful of companies that produce premium pellet grills. The number of entries on this list including the number of corresponding brands is therefore limited. Whatever list of "best grills" you read will likely include more or less the same brands. Again, it's not because these brands are paying critics not to have the competition on their lists, but simply because only a small number of companies are doing this product well. Just like there are only a limited number of companies that do well in supercars or high-end watches.

Reviews - Few products tend to elicit the kind of polarizing appraisals from customers like pellet grills. It's hard to understand exactly why people love or hate them, but it might have something to do with the price. If you're going to drop $8 or $ 800 on an electric pellet smoker, you want and expect it to perform flawlessly. If not, you may well turn to the internet to express your rage. With that said, we certainly do take into account what people say about their pellet grills, but at the ending of the day, as always, our opinions and choices are based primarily on our own experience with these products.

Price - Let's put something aside first: there is no such thing as a "cheap" wood smoker. The price of the items on this list varies between approximately € 400 and € 1,000 and more. That's why we have our eyes open for value when we can find it. In this case, the price-performance ratio is the best price-performance ratio. This is one reason the Green Mountain Grills Davy Crockett Pellet tend Grill tops our list as our top pick. Because it offers an irresistible mix of features at a reasonable price and the quality of artistry guarantees that it will be on your patio for many years to come, it is a value.

Features to Look for in Pellet Grills

When it comes to the cooking mechanics of your choice, pellet grills of meat and garden-fresh produce all share more or less the same characteristics. And of course, all the grills on our list produce exceptional results with a high degree of reliability. What often separates one pellet grill from the other is all of the features. Here are features you'll want to consider when purchasing your pellet grill, along with other practical considerations to keep in mind.

Temperature Control - If you are familiar with cooking, you know the importance of temperature control. Of course, you can always lay a chicken right on a campfire, and in about 10 minutes, you will be able to eat something. But will it be succulent? Will it be juicy and delicious? Of course not. It will be a charred, dry, tasteless piece of meat that no one wants. The fine temperature of your pellet grill allows you to access a wide range of culinary possibilities. It's up to you to choose the fineness you want, but if your grill also allows you to control the meat's internal temperature, even better.

Types of Temperature Controllers - With the above in mind, you will probably want to learn more about pellet grill temperature controllers. Here are some basics:

Three Position Regulators - When you see or hear about a three-position system, it is a system that offers low, medium including high settings. While three settings are better than what you get with charcoal, the control may not be enough for the type of cooking you have in mind.

Multi-position controllers - With a multi-position controller, you can adjust the temperature up or down at 25-degree intervals. This provides a high degree of control than the three-position controllers, and for some people who use their grill primarily for burgers and sausages, it may be sufficient.

PID Regulators - A PID (Proportional Integrative Derivative) regulator incorporates digital technology to maintain a more stable temperature in the grill. Rather than having a continuous cranked auger like most other pellet grills, the PID relies on an algorithm that continually monitors internal temperatures and only releases pellets when circumstances demand it.

Pellet Capacity - No one wants a pellet grill that runs out of fuel halfway through cooking. Therefore, think about the number of people who are likely to attend your parties and meetings, and make sure you buy a grill with a large enough cooking surface and sufficient fuel capacity to keep going until the end. The fuel capacity of the above-profiled pellet grates ranges from 9 to over 20 pounds. Make sure you choose the right capacity to meet your needs.

Heated stand - A heated stand is a great feature to have, especially when dealing with large gatherings. You want to keep in line and make sure everyone's food is good and hot. The heating floors are perfect for this. It's also a nice thing to have when someone asks me, "Can you keep this warm while I go for a swim in the pool?" »Not all wood smokers have a heated grill. So, if that's a feature you're interested in, you're not just assuming that the grill you've got your eye on will have one. Make sure to check it out. Searing Box - In a nutshell, that's what creates these iconic grilling lines on food. Food research also offers contrasts in taste and texture that make the dining experience more complete. Searing foods can also lock in flavors and juices and prevent the meat from turning to dry ash when cooked at high heat.

Additional Considerations The Ease of Use of the Grill - Some of the best pellet grills are plugged in and play business. They also feature automatic temperature control as well as automatic ash cleaning and automatic grease capture and removal. Others require a little more work. If you don't mind cleaning up any drippings or ash yourself or you don't mind buying a separate thermometer to keep the temperature inside the grill and the meat, you can save a few dollars in giving you a simpler grille. If, however, convenience including ease of use is of paramount importance to you, then you'll want to look for features that make it easy to start and clean. Your Budget - Since, as said earlier, pellet grills don't come cheap, you'll want to make sure that the one you've got your eyes on falls within your budget. A few cheaper pellet grills aren't on this list that we wouldn't buy with someone else's money. Why? Because they're so poorly built that they're likely to collapse a year later. In this case, you require going back to your bank account to purchase another. When you are considering a grill, think about the value. In This: A slightly more expensive grill that burns pellets efficiently, is well constructed and meets all of your cooking needs is a better value than an inexpensive grill that ends up on the sidewalk a year after purchase.

CHAPTER 12:

Accessories

Efore you get to the business of grilling and barbecuing, you're going to need some accessories to make things a lot easier for you to deal with. Here are a few:

A Pair of Scissors, and A Set of Knives: These are indispensable. So keep them handy, or buy a new set if your old one is a bit... Meh. You need the knives because you're going to be cutting a lot of meat, whether raw or cooked. You'll also need the scissors to help you out when it comes to trimming choice cuts of your meat, among other preparations you'll be doing. One of the best knives to have would be the 14-inch slicing knife which comes with a hollow edge. This is the best for cutting up large portions of meat, when you're working with poultry, roasts, and briskets.

A Digital Meat Thermometer: Get one of these babies. It's super important, because temperature matters a lot when you're working with meats. I'm not talking about the temperature of your meat on the outside, either. I'm talking about the internal temperatures. You may have a wood pellet smoker grill that has more than a couple of probes, but you should still get yourself another one, so that you can use it to double-check that everything is hunky-dory.

If it so happens that your wood pellet smoker grill did not come with a meat probe, then you cannot do better than one of those barbecue thermometers which work wirelessly and remotely. Invest in a few, because there's no chance you're only grilling one piece of meat all the time. You have to be careful whenever you're putting a thermometer into your meat, whether it's the instant-read kind, or the remote barbecue kind. Always insert the probe into the thickest portions of the meat, and make sure your probe is not in contact with bone.

A Smoker Box: With the smoker box, you could cold smoke various things like jerky, salmon, nuts, meats, and even cheese. If you need something to store your foods in the meantime, and you need it to keep your food warm or at the proper serving temp, then you definitely could use your smoker box for this purpose as well. Go on and contact the manufacturer to check if they can fit your unit with one of these babies. You'll be glad you did!

Searing Grates: There are all sorts of searing grates. It all depends on the make and model of your wood pellet smoker grill. The best thing about searing grates is that you can use them for both direct and indirect flame tech. All you've got to do is contact your manufacturer, so they can let you know the best sort of searing grills that would go with your wood pellet smoker grill. With a searing grate, you get to grill whatever cuts of meat you've got, and you'll end up with some high-quality grills, which once upon a time was the domain of the fanciest of steakhouses only. Open Flame Tech, Flame Zone, Direct Flame: If you've got a good wood pellet smoker grill, then chances are it has the tech that allows you to do your grilling and barbecuing with direct flame. It used to be that you could only do your cooking with indirect flames. However, you cannot grill whatever the heck you want to with direct flame tech, or whatever name the manufacturer of your wood pellet smoker grill has decided to call it (it's all the same thing.) The very best makes will let you grill at temps even higher than 500 degrees Fahrenheit. A Rib Rack: This will let you cook from four slabs to eight slabs of spare ribs at a go. The amount you can cook at any one time would depend on the surface area of your wood pellet smoker grill. A Chicken Wing/Leg Hanger: Want to cook yourself some chicken wings, or legs? Then you're going to need these hangers.

They don't cost much, and you can find them just about anywhere. What they do is they make it easier for the smoke to get into the meat. They also allow the heat to get around your grill as evenly as possible, so that your chicken is properly cooked. Talk about basting with ease!

Barbecue Insulated Gloves: What I love about these gloves is that they are flexible, and light, yet they offer all the protection I need when doing what I do with really hot food as I work. To maintain these, all you have to do is wash them by hand. Please make sure the soap you use to wash them is mild. Then you rinse the gloves, hang them, and let them drip dry. Teflon Coated Fiberglass Mats: these are useful for indirect cooking. It's the only way you can prevent your food from getting all stuck on your precious grill grates. Don't worry, they are approved by the FDA, and are very safe for your dishwasher.

Some accessories are essential and are must-haves to have a fantastic experience with Wood Pellet Grill Smokers. There are several grilling accessories in their thousands; however, there are certain ones that are non-negotiable if you want to get the best from your Pellet Smoker.

Grilling Tools

Some tools are specially designed for grilling purposes. They are usually more robust and sturdier than regular kitchen utensils. Some of these tools include; spatula, tongs, fork, etc.

Heat-resistant Gloves

Everyone loves having a barbecue party. But while you are at it, you want to make sure you do not burn your hands. Getting a pair of heat-resistant gloves will go a long way to protect you from the fire's scorching heat.

Basting Brush and the Sauce Mop

These tools are essential to prevent dry-out. When grilling, the tools help to add moisture after the barbecue has formed its crust. The brush usually has a long handle, and it's made of silicone for easy cleaning. The sauce mop is more like a bunch of strings attached to a long handle. It becomes easy to reach the pellet smoker's back with the sauce mop without the risk of burns.

Grill Brush

This tool is essential to keep your cooking area clean. It is recommended to use this after every cook to remove any bristle stuck on your grill grate. Ensure to crank the temperature for about 10 minutes before the cleaning is done.

Cutting Board

A quality cutting board is an essential tool to have as well. It will create a strong base for you to handle your brisket, however large the size is.

Several other helpful tools and accessories are available, although they may not be considered significant. When you invest in the right accessories, they make your grilling experience a smooth and enjoyable one.

CHAPTER 13:

Smoking, Grilling, Cooking, Baking On Your Grill

A Little hard-core research reveals that some companies are still in business today that might appear to have the first to offer the first pellet-style smokers to the open market. Dating back to the early 1980s, these companies first experimented with wood pellets as fuel for barbecue smokers. As they progressed with the designs, many successful grills were built and tested, and the rest was history. Today, the most notable brands of Pellet Smoker Grills are as follows:

Green Mountain

Yoder Smokers

Mak Grills

Fast Eddy's Cookshack Grills

So, what exactly is a wood Pellet Smoker Grill? Here are the basics of a good high-quality wood pellet smoker. Generally, the higher the temperature gauge is set, the more pellets get dispensed into the auger. After the pellets are delivered into the fire pot, a red-hot rod will ignite them, starting the flames. A fan then keeps a gentle airflow across the fire area that creates a convection oven type of heat that cooks your food nicely and evenly. A drip tray is located just over the fire pot to keep you clear of any direct flame activity. This tray also catches any subsequent drippings to help prevent unwanted flare-ups.

The design technology behind wood Pellet Smoker Grills is not new, really, but the grills are indeed making a lively splash in the grill markets. People are asking if these types of grills are safe to use. The answer is yes. Food-grade wood pellets are not any riskier than any other food prep choices.

The wood pellets used in pellet smokers are exclusive to that task. This is because they produce less than 1% ash. As an example, if you use an entire 40-pound bag of pellets in your smoker, unbelievably, you will only have ½ of a cup of ash, which is only half a cup for 40 lb. Bag. In addition to this, they provide diners with gigantic flavor per capita and no worries about the need to watch the levels of air to fuel mixture, like you would when be using wood chips or wood chunks.

How does the Heat Distribution work in Pellet Smoker Grills?

A heat shield that covers the firebox works to distribute the heat to both sides of the grill. This causes the air to flow up into the convection-style grill chamber. Then, a sensor that is conveniently mounted on the inside of the grill sends data electronically to the on-board computer at the amazing rate of 10 times per second, and the controller then adjusts both the airflow and the pellet distribution mechanism to maintain the temperature that you set.

Why Pellet Grills?

By utilizing hardwood pellets, the meat product gets infused with a real woodsy, smoky flavor. The new Pellet Smoker Grills can be relied on to do the work on their own, as they are set up to be automatic by the user.

The main and most obvious difference is that they provide the user with an automated air and fuel delivery system, making a pellet grill much easier to control temperatures and relax while doing it.

So, if you thought that smokers are just too difficult to control cooking temperatures, well think again. Pellet grills simply remove the fuss and worry that traditional smokers require, making them virtually a "set it and forget it" way to grill.

Pellet grills give you even more as if that were not enough. With your new pellet grill, you have the absolute convenience of combining several varied cooking options. Old-time smokers only smoke their food, so if you want to grill, bake, and roast your food, you would need to purchase separate units for each process.

Pellet Grills are different than propane or gas grills in that they offer more control. Pellet grills and gas grills both offer their own set of convenient features to the outdoor chef but look more closely, and you will see some major differences. Gas grills are very good when cooking chores, but due to poor insulation, they do not typically perform very well at all at low cooking temperatures. Also, the older style of propane grills needs to be set up so that they receive the proper degree of ventilation. This, alone, makes them a poor choice for smokers. The Pellet Grill is a no-brainer in today's world!

Pellet grills provide the chef with more flavor options. With pellet grills, the wood pellets are available in many different flavors. This provides you with the ability to cook all the foods on your Pellet Smoker Grill. In the end, sure, they both cook your food, but the pellet grill is exponentially better on so many levels. For me, there is no choice but the Pellet Smoker Grill!

Then there is the question of using a Pellet Grill or staying with the highly coveted charcoal method of barbecuing your fine foods.

Charcoal grills have long been considered the king of the backyard barbecue area. There are several choices of configurations for charcoal grills but with two choices for fuel: lump charcoal or charcoal briquettes. Grilling using a charcoal grill is definitely a labor of love. I know several people who defend them to the ends of the earth, and that's fine. We are all different, and thank goodness for that, too. But cooking on a charcoal grill is really not so easy. It takes quite a lot of practice to get all the elements just right and it is difficult to control temperatures.

Another consideration would be to pit the Pellet Smoker Grills up to the already well-established Electric Smoker available everywhere in the backyard cooking market. Today's electric smokers are actually modern takes on classic smokers and offer lots of control. Electric smokers heat wood chips to get good results. They are quite convenient to operate and allow the chef in your family to set it and forget it. The problem arises when you need to grill and sear. For that, you need very high temperatures, generally between 450 and 550 degrees. Electric smokers do get hot enough for most cooking chores, so it is not all bad news.

CHAPTER 14:

Know Your Meats

Choose the type of meat that tastes good with a smoky flavor. Following meat goes well for smoking.

Beef: ribs, brisket, and corned beef.

Pork: spareribs, roast, shoulder, and ham.

Poultry: whole chicken, whole turkey, and big game hens.

Seafood: Salmon, scallops, trout, and lobster.

Brine is a solution to treating poultry, pork, or ham. It involves dissolving brine ingredients in water poured into a huge container and then adding meat to it. Then let soak for at least 8 hours and after that, rinse it well and pat dry before you begin smoking.

Marinate treat beef or briskets and add flavors to it. It is better to make deep cuts in meat to let marinate ingredients deep into it. Drain meat or smoke it straightaway.

Rubs are commonly used to treat beef, poultry, or ribs. They are a combination of salt and many spices, rubbed generously all over the meat. Then the meat is left to rest for at least 2 hours or more before smoking it.

Before smoking meat, make sure it is at room Smoke Temperature. This ensures the meat is cooked evenly and reaches its internal Smoke Temperature at the end of smoking time.

Placing Meat into the Smoker

Do not place the meat directly overheat into the smoker because the main purpose of smoking is cooking meat at a low Smoke Temperature. Set aside your fuel on one side of the smoker and place the meat on the other side and let cook.

Smoking time: The smoking time of meat depends on the internal Smoke Temperature. For this, use a meat thermometer and insert it into the thickest part of the meat. The smoking time also varies with the size of the meat. Check recipes to determine the exact smoking time for the meat.

Find the Right Smoke Temperature

There are two ways to smoke meat that is cold smoking and hot smoking. In cold smoking, meat is cooked between 68 to 86 degrees F until smoked but moist. It is a good choice to smoke meat like chicken breast, steak, beef, pork chops, salmon, and cheese. The cold smoking concern with adding flavor to the meat rather than cooking. Therefore, when the meat is cold smoked, it should be cured, baked, or steamed before serving.

On the other hand, hot smoking cooks the meat completely, in addition, to enhance its flavor. Therefore, meat should be a cook until its internal Smoke Temperature is between 126 to 176 degrees F. Do not let meat Smoke Temperature reach 185 degrees F as at this Smoke Temperature, meat shrinks or buckles. Large meat cuts like brisket, ham, ribs and pulled pork turn out great when hot smoked.

CHAPTER 15:

Pork

1. Cocoa Crusted Pork Tenderloin
Preparation Time: 30 Minutes
Cooking Time: 25 Minutes
Servings: 5
Ingredients:
- One pork tenderloin
- 1/2 tbsp fennel, ground
- 2 tbsp cocoa powder, unsweetened
- 1 tbsp smoked paprika
- 1/2 tbsp kosher salt
- 1/2 tbsp black pepper
- 1 tbsp extra virgin olive oil
- Three green onion

Directions:
1. Remove the silver skin and the tissues from the pork loin.
2. Combine the remaining ingredients in a mixing bowl, then rub the mixture on the pork. Refrigerate for 30 minutes.
3. Preheat the wood pellet grill for 15 minutes with the lid closed.
4. Sear all sides of the loin at the front of the grill, then lessen the temperature to 350°F then put the pork on the center grill.
5. Cook the pork for 15 more minutes or until the temperature is 145°F.

6. When done, let the meat cool for 10 minutes before slicing it. Enjoy

Nutrition:

Calories 264 Total fat 13.1g

Saturated fat 6g Total Carbs 4.6g

Net Carbs 1.2g Protein 33g

Sugar 0g Fiber 3.4g Sodium: 66mg

2. Wood Pellet Grilled Bacon

Preparation Time: 30 Minutes

Cooking Time: 25 Minutes

Servings: 6

Ingredients:

- 1 lb. Bacon, thickly cut

Directions:

1. Preheat your wood pellet grill to 375°F.
2. Line a baking sheet with parchment paper, then place the bacon on it in a single layer.
3. Close the lid, then bake it for 20 minutes. Flip over, close the top, and bake for an additional 5 minutes.
4. Serve with the favorite side and enjoy it.

Nutrition:

Calories 315

Total fat 14g

Saturated fat 10g

Protein 9g

Sodium: 500mg

3. Wood Pellet Grilled Pork Chops

Preparation Time: 20 Minutes

Cooking Time: 10 Minutes

Servings: 6

Ingredients:

- Six pork chops, thickly cut
- BBQ rub

Directions:

1. Preheat the wood pellet to 450°F.
2. Season the pork chops using the BBQ rub.
3. Put the pork chops on the grill and cook for 6 minutes or until the temperature reaches 145°F
4. Remove the pork from the grill, then let sit for 10 minutes before serving.
5. Enjoy.

Nutrition:

Calories 264

Total fat 13g

Saturated fat 6g

Total Carbs 4g

Net Carbs 1g

Protein 33g

Fiber 3g

Sodium: 66mg

4. Wood Pellet Blackened Pork Chops

Preparation Time: 5 Minutes

Cooking Time: 20 Minutes

Servings: 6

Ingredients:

- Six pork chops
- 1/4 cup blackening seasoning
- Salt and pepper to taste

Directions:

1. Preheat your grill to 375°F.
2. Meanwhile, generously season the pork chops with the blackening seasoning, salt, and pepper.
3. Put the pork chops on the grill and close the lid.
4. Let grill for 8 minutes, then flip the chops. Cook until the internal temperature reaches 142°F.
5. Remove the pork from the grill. Let it cool for 10 minutes. Then you may begin slicing it.
6. Serve and enjoy.

Nutrition:

Calories 333

Total fat 18g

Saturated fat 6g

Total Carbs 1g

Protein 40g,

Fiber 1g

Sodium: 3175mg

CHAPTER 16:

Beef

5. Smoked Trip Tip with Java Chophouse
Preparation Time: 10 Minutes
Cooking Time: 90 Minutes
Servings: 4
Ingredients:
- 2 tbsp olive oil
- 2 tbsp java chophouse seasoning
- 3 lb. Trip tip roast, fat cap, and silver skin removed

Directions:
1. Startup your wood pellet grill and smoker and set the temperature to 225°F.
2. Rub the roast with olive oil and seasoning, then place it on the smoker rack.
3. Smoke until the internal temperature is 140°F.
4. Remove the tri-tip from the smoker and let rest for 10 minutes before serving. Enjoy.

Nutrition:
Calories 270
Total fat 7g
Total Carbs 0g
Protein 23g
Sodium: 47mg
Potassium 289mg

6. Supper Beef Roast

Preparation Time: 5 Minutes
Cooking Time: 3 Hours
Servings: 7
Ingredients:

- 3-1/2 beef top round
- 3 tbsp vegetable oil
- Prime rib rub
- 2 cups beef broth
- One russet potato, peeled and sliced
- Two carrots, peeled and sliced
- Two celery stalks, chopped
- One onion, sliced
- Two thyme sprigs

Directions:

1. Rub the roast with vegetable oil and place it on the roasting fat side up. Season with prime rib rub then pours the beef broth.
2. Put the temperature to 500°F and preheat the wood pellet grill for 15 minutes with the lid closed.
3. Cook for 30 minutes or until the roast is well seared.
4. Reduce temperature to 225°F. Add the veggies and thyme and cover with foil. Cook for three more hours or until the temperature reaches 135°F
5. Take away the meat from the grill and let it sit for 10 minutes. Slice it and serve with vegetables and the pan drippings.
6. Enjoy.

Nutrition:

Calories 697
Total fat 10g
Total Carbs 127g
Protein 34g
Sugar 14g
Fiber 22g
Sodium: 3466mgPotassium 2329mg

7. Wood Pellet Grill Deli-Style Roast Beef
Preparation Time: 15 Minutes
Cooking Time: 4 Hours
Servings: 2
Ingredients:

- 4lb round-bottomed roast
- 1 tbsp coconut oil
- 1/4 tbsp garlic powder
- 1/4 tbsp onion powder
- 1/4 tbsp thyme
- 1/4 tbsp oregano
- 1/2 tbsp paprika
- 1/2 tbsp salt
- 1/2 tbsp black pepper

Directions:

1. Combine all the dry hubs to get a dry rub.
2. Roll the roast in foil, then coat with the rub.
3. Set your grill to 185°F and place the roast on the grill.
4. Smoke for 4 hours or until the internal temperature reaches 140°F.
5. Remove the roast, then allow it to cool for 10 minutes.
6. Slice thinly and serve.

Nutrition:
Calories 90
Total fat 3g
Total Carbs 0g
Protein 14g
Sodium: 420mg

8. Beef Tenderloin

Preparation Time: 10 minutes

Cooking Time: 1 hour 19 minutes

Servings: 12

Ingredients:

- 1 (5-pound) beef tenderloin, trimmed
- Kosher salt, as required
- ¼ cup olive oil
- Freshly ground black pepper, as required

Directions:

1. With kitchen strings, tie the tenderloin at 7-8 places.
2. Season tenderloin with kosher salt generously.
3. With a plastic wrap, cover the tenderloin and keep aside at room temperature for about 1 hour.
4. Preheat the Wood Pellet Grill & Smoker on grill setting to 225-250 degrees F.
5. Now, coat tenderloin with oil evenly and season with black pepper.
6. Arrange tenderloin onto the grill and cook for about 55-65 minutes.
7. Now, place cooking grate directly over hot coals and sear tenderloin for about 2 minutes per side.

Nutrition:

Calories 425

Total Fat 21.5 g

Saturated Fat 7.2 g

Cholesterol 174 mg

Sodium 123 mg Total Carbs 0 g

Fiber 0 g Sugar 0 g Protein 54.7 g

CHAPTER 17:

Turkey

9. Herb Roasted Turkey

Preparation Time: 15 Minutes
Cooking Time: 3 Hours and 30 Minutes
Servings: 12
Ingredients:

- 14 pounds' turkey, cleaned
- 2 tablespoons chopped mixed herbs
- Pork and poultry rub as needed
- ¼ teaspoon ground black pepper
- 3 tablespoons butter, unsalted, melted
- 8 tablespoons butter, unsalted, softened
- 2 cups chicken broth

Directions:

1. Clean the turkey by removing the giblets, wash it inside out, pat dry with paper towels, then place it on a roasting pan and tuck the turkey wings by tiring with butcher's string.
2. Switch on the Traeger grill, fill the grill hopper with hickory flavored wood pellets, power the grill on by using the control panel, select 'smoke' on the temperature dial,
3. Meanwhile, prepared herb butter and for this, take a small bowl, place the softened butter in it, add black pepper and mixed herbs and beat until fluffy.

4. Place some of the prepared herb butter underneath the skin of turkey by using a handle of a wooden spoon, and massage the skin to distribute butter evenly.

5. Then rub the exterior of the turkey with melted butter, season with pork and poultry rub, and pour the broth in the roasting pan.

6. When the grill has preheated, open the lid, place roasting pan containing turkey on the grill grate, shut the grill and smoke for 3 hours and 30 minutes until the internal temperature reaches 165 degrees F and the top has turned golden brown.

7. When done, transfer turkey to a cutting board, let it rest for 30 minutes, then carve it into slices and serve.

Nutrition: Calories: 154.6 Fat: 3.1 g Carbs: 8.4 g Protein: 28.8 g

10. Turkey Legs

Preparation Time: 10 Minutes

Cooking Time: 5 Hours

Servings: 4

Ingredients:

- 4 turkey legs
- For the Brine:
- ½ cup curing salt
- 1 tablespoon whole black peppercorns
- 1 cup BBQ rub
- ½ cup brown sugar
- 2 bay leaves
- 2 teaspoons liquid smoke
- 16 cups of warm water
- 4 cups ice
- 8 cups of cold water

Directions:

1. Prepare the brine and for this, take a large stockpot, place it over high heat, pour warm water in it, add peppercorn, bay leaves, and liquid smoke, stir in salt, sugar, and BBQ rub and bring it to a boil.

2. Remove pot from heat, bring it to room temperature, then pour in cold water, add ice cubes and let the brine chill in the refrigerator.

3. Then add turkey legs in it, submerge them completely, and let soak for 24 hours in the refrigerator.

4. After 24 hours, remove turkey legs from the brine, rinse well and pat dry with paper towels.

5. When ready to cook, switch on the Traeger grill, fill the grill hopper with hickory flavored wood pellets, power the grill on by using the control panel, select 'smoke' on the temperature dial, or set the temperature to 250 degrees F and let it preheat for a minimum of 15 minutes.

6. When the grill has preheated, open the lid, place turkey legs on the grill grate, shut the grill, and smoke for 5 hours until nicely browned and the internal temperature reaches 165 degrees F. Serve immediately.

Nutrition: Calories: 416 Fat: 13.3 g Carbs: 0 g Protein: 69.8 g

CHAPTER 18:

Poultry

11. Buffalo Wings

Preparation Time: 10 minutes

Cooking Time: 53 Minutes

Servings: 8

Ingredients:

Ingredient for Chicken Wings:

- 4 pounds of Chicken Wings
- 2 teaspoons of Corn Starch
- 2 tablespoons of buffalo wings rub
- Salt, To Taste

Ingredients for Buffalo Sauce:

- 1/3 cup Spicy Mustard
- 1 Cup Franks Red Hot Sauce
- 8 tablespoons of Unsalted Butter

Side:

- 1 cup Blue cheese dressing

Directions:

1. Preheat the grill to 375 degrees F, for 15 minutes.
2. Meanwhile, the grill is preheating add wings to a large bowl and sprinkle corn starch, spice rub, and salt.
3. Mix the ingredients well.
4. When the grill is heated, place the wings on the grill and cook for 38 minutes.
5. Meanwhile, in a bowl, mix all the buffalo sauce ingredients.

6. Put the sauce over the wings and then cook the wings for additional 15 minutes with the lid closed.
7. Serve the wings with blue cheese dressing.
8. Enjoy.

Nutrition: Calories: 193; Total Fat: 13 g; Saturated Fat: 6.5 g; Protein: 17 g; Carbs: 2 g; Fiber: 4 g; Sugar: 0 g

12. Herbed Smoked Hen

Preparation Time: 10 minutes

Cooking Time: 50 Minutes

Servings: 5

Ingredients:

- 12 cups of filtered water
- 3 cups of beer nonalcoholic
- Sea Salt, to taste
- ⅓ Cup brown sugar
- 2 tablespoons of rosemary
- ½ teaspoon of sage
- 2.5 pounds of a whole chicken, trimmed and giblets removed
- 6 tablespoons of butter
- 2 tablespoons of Olive oil, for basting
- 1/3 cup Italian seasoning
- 1 tablespoon garlic powder
- 1 tablespoon of lemon zest

Directions:

1. Transfer water in a large cooking pot and then add sugar and salt to the water.
2. Boil the water until the sugar and salt dissolve.
3. Now to the boiling water, add rosemary and sage.
4. Boil it until aroma comes.
5. Now pour the beer into the water and then submerge the chicken into the boiling water.
6. Turn off the heat and refrigerate the chicken for a few hours.
7. After few hours removed it from the brine, and then pat dry with the paper towel.
8. Let the chicken sit for a limited minutes at room temperature.
9. Now rub the chicken with the butter and massage it completely for fine coating.
10. Season the chicken with garlic powder, lemon zest, and Italian seasoning.

11. Preheat the Electrical smoker at 270 degrees Fahrenheit until the smoke started to build.

12. Baste the chicken with olive oil and put it on the grill grate.

13. Cook the chicken with the lid closed, for 30 to 40 minutes, or until the internal temperature reaches 165 degrees F.

14. Serve and enjoy.

Nutrition: Calories: 153; Total Fat: 16 g; Saturated Fat: 16.5 g; Protein: 15 g; Carbs: 3 g; Fiber: 0 g; Sugar: 5 g

13. Smoked Chicken Thighs

Preparation Time: 10 minutes

Cooking Time: 2 Hours

Servings: 4

Ingredients:

- 2.5 pounds of chicken thighs
- 4 tablespoons soy sauce
- 4 teaspoons sesame oil
- 2 garlic cloves
- 1-inch ginger, grated
- 1 small white onion, chopped
- ½ tablespoon thyme
- 2 teaspoons allspice, powder
- ½ teaspoon cinnamon
- ½ teaspoon crushed red chili peppers, powder

Directions:

1. Take a food processor and add soya sauce, sesame oil, garlic cloves, ginger, onions, thyme, allspice powder, cinnamon, and red chili peppers.
2. Blend the mixture into a smooth paste.
3. Coat the chicken thighs with the blended paste, and marinate in a zip-lock plastic bag for 2 hours in the refrigerator.
4. Preheat the smoker at 225 degrees F, until the smoke started to form.
5. Place the chicken directly onto the grill grate, and cook the chicken for 2 hours.
6. Once the temperature reaches 145 degrees Fahrenheit, the chicken is ready to be served
7. Remove the chicken from the gill great, and let it sit at the room temperature for 20 minutes, before serving.
8. Serve and enjoy.

Nutrition: Calories: 267; Total Fat: 19 g; Saturated Fat: 4.5 g; Protein: 29 g; Carbs: 20 g; Fiber: 0 g; Sugar: 0 g

14. Maple Glazed Whole Chicken

Preparation Time: 10 minutes

Cooking Time: 3 Hours

Servings: 4

Ingredients:

Ingredients for The Rub:

- Black pepper and salt, to taste
- 3 garlic cloves, minced
- 3 teaspoons of onion powder
- 1.5 teaspoons of ginger, minced
- ½ teaspoon of five-spice powder

Basic Ingredients

- 2.5 pounds' whole chicken
- 4 tablespoons of melted butter
- 1 cup of grapefruit juice
- 2.5 cups chicken stock

Ingredients for The Glaze:

- 6 teaspoons of coconut milk
- 3 tablespoons of sesame oil
- 3 tablespoons of maple syrup
- 1 tablespoon of lemon juice
- 4 tablespoons of melted butter

Directions:

1. In a small cooking pot, pour the coconut milk and add sesame oil, maple syrup, melted butter, and lemon juice.
2. Reserve some of the mixture for further use.
3. Take a separate cooking pot and add chicken stock, butter, and grapefruit juice.
4. Submerge the chicken completely in the brain and let it sit for a few hours for marinating.
5. In a separate bowl, combine all the rub ingredients.
6. After a few hours pass, take out the chicken from the liquid and pat dry with a paper towel.

7. Now cover the chicken with the rub mixture.
8. Preheat the smoker grill for 20 minutes at 225 degrees Fahrenheit.
9. Cherry or apple wood chip can be used to create the smoke.
10. Place chicken onto the smoker grill grate and cook for 3 hours by closing the lid.
11. After every 30 minutes, baste the chicken with the maple glaze.
12. Once the internal temperature of the chicken reaches 165 degrees Fahrenheit the chicken is ready to be served.
13. Remove the chicken from the grill grate and baste it with the glaze and additional butter on top.
14. Let the chicken sit at the room temperature for 10 minutes before cutting and serving.

Nutrition: Calories: 227; Total Fat: 14 g; Saturated Fat: 4.5 g; Protein: 17 g; Carbs: 8 g; Fiber: 0 g; Sugar: 2 g

15. Sriracha Chicken Wings

Preparation Time: 10 minutes

Cooking Time: 2 Hours

Servings: 4

Ingredients:

- 2 pounds of chicken wings
- 2 teaspoons garlic powder
- Sea salt, to taste
- Freshly ground black pepper, to taste
- Ingredients for The Sauce:
- 1/3 cup raw honey
- 1/3 cup Sriracha sauce
- 2 tablespoons coconut amino
- 3 limes, juice only

Directions:

1. Take a huge mixing bowl and combine the sauce ingredients including Sriracha sauce, raw honey, coconut amino, and lime juice.
2. Using chicken, rub the chicken with salt, black pepper, and garlic powder.
3. Preheat the smoker grill for 30 minutes at 225 degrees F.
4. Put the chicken directly onto the grill grate and smoke with the close lid for 2 hours.
5. Remove the chicken from the grill grate and dumped into the sauce bowl.
6. Toss the chicken wings well for the fine coating.
7. Serve and Enjoy.

Nutrition: Calories: 107; Total Fat: 10 g; Saturated Fat: 0.9 g; Protein: 15 g; Carbs: 3 g; Fiber: 0 g; Sugar: 0 g

CHAPTER 19:

Fish and Seafood

16. Grilled Oysters with Veggie Sauce
Preparation Time: 20 Minutes
Cooking Time: 25 Minutes
Servings: 4
Ingredients:

- Five tablespoons extra-virgin olive oil
- Two medium onions, chopped
- One medium red bell pepper, chopped
- Two lemons, juiced
- Three dried bay leaves
- Five tablespoons minced garlic
- Three tablespoons Traeger Chicken Rub
- Three teaspoons dried thyme
- ¼ cup white wine
- Five tablespoons hot pepper sauce
- Three tablespoons Worcestershire Sauce
- Four butter sticks
- 12 whole oysters, cleaned and shucked
- Italian cheese blend, as needed

Directions:

1. When ready to cook, put the Traeger to High and preheat, lid closed for 15 minutes.
2. In a pan, cook the olive oil over medium heat. Then add the bell peppers, onions, lemon juice, bay leaves, garlic, Traeger

Chicken Rub, and thyme to the pan. Sauté the vegetable mixture for 5 to 7 minutes, or until the onions are translucent and peppers are tender.

3. Add the white wine, hot pepper sauce, Worcestershire Sauce, and butter to the pan. Sauté for another 15 minutes.
4. Place the oysters and top with the sauce—Cook for 5 minutes.
5. Top with Italian cheese and serve hot.

Nutrition:

Calories 261 Total fat 14g

Saturated fat 5g Total carbs 5g

Net carbs 5g Protein 28g

Sodium 1238mg

17. Crispy Fried Halibut Fish Sticks

Preparation Time: 10 Minutes

Cooking Time: 3 to 4 Minutes

Servings: 4

Ingredients:

- Extra-virgin olive oil, as needed
- 1½ pounds (680 g) halibut, rinsed, patted dry, and cut into 1-inch strips
- ½ cup all-purpose flour
- 1½ teaspoons salt
- One teaspoon ground black pepper
- Two large eggs
- 1½ cups panko bread crumbs
- Two tablespoons dried parsley
- One teaspoon dried dill weed

Directions:

1. When ready to cook, put Traeger temperature to 500°f (260°c) and preheat, lid closed for 15 minutes.
2. Put a Dutch oven inside the grill to preheat for about 10 minutes, with enough olive oil to fry the fish.
3. In a bowl, blend the all-purpose flour, salt, and pepper.
4. In a separate bowl, beat the eggs. In another bowl, combine the panko, parsley, and dill.
5. Dredge the fish fillets in the flour mixture, then the eggs, and then the panko mixture.
6. Place the coated fish fillets in the oil and fry for around 3 to 4 minutes, or wait until they reach an internal temperature of 130°f (54°c).
7. Serve warm.

Nutrition:

Calories 245 Total fat 2g

Total carbs 2g Protein 52g

Sugars 1g

Fiber 1g Sodium 442mg

18. White Fish Steaks with Orange Basil Pesto

Preparation Time: 10 Minutes

Cooking Time: 15 Minutes

Servings: 4

Ingredients:

- One orange, juiced
- 2 cups fresh basil
- 1 cup chopped flat-leaf parsley
- ½ cup toasted walnuts
- Two teaspoons orange zest
- ½ cup olive oil
- 1 cup grated Parmesan cheese
- Four white fish steaks rinsed and patted dry
- ½ teaspoon coarse sea salt
- ½ teaspoon black pepper

Directions:

1. In a food processor, blend the orange juice, basil, parsley, walnuts, and orange zest and pulse until finely chopped. While the machine is working, gradually drizzle in the olive oil until the mixture is emulsified.
2. Scrape the pesto into a bowl and mix in the Parmesan cheese.
3. Brush the fish steaks with olive oil on both sides and season with salt and pepper.
4. Position the fish steaks on the grill grate. Grill for 12 to 15 minutes, turning once with a thin-bladed metal spatula, or until the fish is opaque and breaks into chunks when pressed with a fork.
5. Transfer the steaks to a platter. Drizzle with the prepared pesto and serve immediately.

Nutrition:

Calories 245 Total fat 2g

Total carbs 2g Protein 52g

Sugars 1g Fiber 1g

Sodium 442mg

19. Lemony Salmon Fillets

Preparation Time: 10 Minutes

Cooking Time: 20 Minutes

Servings: 2

Ingredients:

- Two tablespoons butter softened
- Two teaspoons fresh chopped dill, plus more for garnish
- One teaspoon lemon juice
- ½ teaspoon lemon zest
- ½ teaspoon salt
- Black pepper, to taste
- 4 (8-ounce / 227-g) salmon fillets, skin on
- One lemon, thinly sliced

Directions:

1. When fit to cook, set Traeger temperature to 350°f (177°c) and preheat for 15 minutes.
2. Meanwhile, stir together all the ingredients, except for the salmon and lemon, in a bowl.
3. Generously spread the lemon-dill butter over the top of the salmon fillets and top with a slice of lemon.
4. Place the salmon fillets on the grill grate, skin-side facing down. Cook for 15 to 20 minutes, for a medium-rare salmon, or until the salmon is done to your liking.
5. Serve garnished with the fresh dill.

CHAPTER 20:

Lamb

20. Roasted Rack of Lamb

Preparation time: 10 minutes **Cooking Time: 5 Hours Servings: 2**

Ingredients:

- 1 Rack (1-1/2 Lbs.) Lamb, Frenched
- 1/2 Cup Yellow Mustard
- 1 Tablespoon Salt
- 1 Teaspoon Black Pepper, Ground
- 1 Cup Panko
- 1 Tablespoon Italian Parsley, Minced
- 1 Teaspoon Sage, Minced
- 1 Teaspoon Rosemary, Minced

Directions:

1. Shapely and clean the lamb if your butcher hasn't already done so. Rub the exterior with mustard and season generously with salt and pepper. In a narrow baking dish, combine breadcrumbs and herbs. Dredge the lamb in the breadcrumb mixture. Start the Traeger grill on Smoke with the lid open until the fire is established (4 to 5 minutes). Place the temperature to 450 degrees F and preheat lid closed for 10-15 minutes. Put the rack of lamb directly on the grill grate bone side down and cook for 20 minutes or until the internal temperature reaches 120 degrees F when an instant read thermometer is inserted into the thickest part of the lamb.

Nutrition:

Calories: 110 Carbohydrates: 19 g Protein: 29 g Sodium: 15 mg Cholesterol: 59 mg

21. Grilled Butterflied Leg of Lamb

Preparation time: 20 minutes
Cooking Time: 5 Hours
Servings: 2
Ingredients:

- 1 Lemon, Juiced and Rinds Reserved
- 1/4 Cup Red Wine Vinegar
- 4 Cloves Garlic, Minced
- 2 Tablespoon Fresh or 2 Teaspoon Dried Rosemary, Minced
- 2 Teaspoon Fresh, or 1 Teaspoon Dried Fresh Thyme, Minced
- 1 Teaspoon Salt
- 1 Teaspoon Black Pepper, Freshly Ground
- 1 Cup Extra-Virgin Olive Oil
- 1 Onion, Sliced into Rings
- 1 (4-5 Lbs.) Leg of Lamb, Butterflied and Boneless

Directions:

1. For the Marinade: Slice the lemon into quarters and get rid of the seeds.
2. Squeeze lemon juice into a mixing bowl and reserve the lemon rinds.
3. Add the red wine vinegar, garlic, rosemary, thyme, salt and pepper and stir until the salt crystals dissolve. Whisk in the olive oil. Get rid of any netting from the lamb. Set the lamb into a large resealable plastic bag.
4. Transfer marinade into the bag
5. Take away the lamb from the marinade and pat dry with paper towels. Discard the marinade.
6. Start the Traeger according to grill instructions.
7. Set the temperature to High and preheat, lid closed, for 10 to 15 minutes. Organize the lamb on the grill grate, fat-side down.
8. Grill for 15 to 20 minutes per side or until the internal temperature reaches 135 degrees F for medium-rare.

Nutrition: Calories: 120 Carbohydrates: 39 g Protein: 39 g Sodium: 15 mg Cholesterol: 59 mg

22. Braised Irish Lamb Stew

Preparation time: 10 minutes
Cooking Time: 5 Hours
Servings: 3
Ingredients:

- 4 Lbs. Lamb Shoulder, Boneless, Cut into 1-Inch Pieces
- Salt and Pepper, To Taste
- 1/4 Cup Flour
- 1/4 Cup Butter, Room Temp
- 8 Oz Bacon, Chopped
- 2 Cloves Garlic, Minced
- 1/2 Cup White Wine
- 4 Cups Beef Stock
- 2 Bay Leaf
- 2 Sprigs Thyme
- 1 Sprig Rosemary
- 1 Onion, Small Dice
- 2 Carrots, Peeled, Cut into 1/2-Inch Pieces
- 2 Large Potatoes, Peeled, 1/2-Inch Dice

Directions:

1. Start the Traeger on Smoke with the lid open until the fire is established (4 to 5 minutes). Set the temperature to 350 degrees F and preheat, lid closed, for 10-15 minutes.
2. Season lamb with salt and pepper. Heat 2 Tablespoon olive oil in a Dutch oven over medium heat.
3. Add bacon and cook 15-20 minutes mix occasionally until lightly browned.
4. Remove bacon and discard all but 2 Tablespoon of the bacon fat.
5. Put fat back to the Dutch oven and onions and sauté until translucent. Add garlic and cook 30 seconds more.
6. Add stock, herbs, potatoes and carrots and bring to a simmer. Cover and transfer to the grill. Let stew cook for 1-1/2 to 2 hours or until the lamb is tender and falling apart.

7. Remove stew from grill and place back on the stove top over medium heat. Mix butter and flour together in a small bowl and whisk into the stew. Let cook 5-10 minutes or until the stew is thick enough to coat the back of a spoon.

8. Season with salt and pepper to taste. Remove bay leaves and springs from thyme and rosemary and serve. Enjoy!

Nutrition:

Calories: 120 Carbohydrates: 39 g

Protein: 39 g

Sodium: 15 mg

Cholesterol: 59 mg

CHAPTER 21:

Vegetables

23. Wood Pellet Grill Spicy Sweet Potatoes

Preparation Time: 10 Minutes
Cooking Time: 35 Minutes
Servings: 6
Ingredients:

- 2 lb. Sweet potatoes, cut into chunks
- One red onion, chopped
- 2 tbsp oil
- 2 tbsp orange juice
- 1 tbsp roasted cinnamon
- 1 tbsp salt
- 1/4 tbsp Chipotle chili pepper

Directions:

1. Preheat the wood pellet grill to 425°F with the lid closed.
2. Toss the sweet potatoes with onion, oil, and juice.
3. In a mixing bowl, mix cinnamon, salt, and pepper, then sprinkle the mixture over the sweet potatoes.
4. Spread the potatoes on a lined baking dish in a single layer.
5. Place the baking dish in the grill and grill for 30 minutes or until the sweet potatoes are tender.
6. Serve and enjoy.

Nutrition: Calories 145 Total fat 5g Total Carbs 23g Protein 2g Sugar 3g Fiber 4g Sodium: 428mg Potassium 230mg

24. Wood Pellet Smoked Vegetables

Preparation Time: 5 Minutes

Cooking Time: 15 Minutes

Servings: 6

Ingredients:

- One ear corn, fresh, husks and silk strands removed
- 1yellow squash, sliced
- One red onion, cut into wedges
- One green pepper, cut into strips
- One red pepper, cut into strips
- One yellow pepper, cut into strips
- 1 cup mushrooms, halved
- 2 tbsp oil
- 2 tbsp chicken seasoning

Directions:

1. Soak the pecan wood pellets in water for an hour. Remove the pellets from the water and fill the smoker box with the wet pellets.
2. Place the smoker box under the grill and close the lid. Heat the grill on high heat for 10 minutes or until smoke starts coming out from the wood chips.
3. Meanwhile, toss the veggies in oil and seasonings, then transfer them into a grill basket.
4. Grill for 10 minutes while turning occasionally. Serve and enjoy.

Nutrition:

Calories 97

Total fat 5g

Total Carbs 11g

Protein 2g

Sugar 1g

Fiber 3g

Sodium: 251mg

Potassium 171mg

25. Vegan Smoked Carrot Dogs

Preparation Time: 25 Minutes

Cooking Time: 35 Minutes

Servings: 4

Ingredients:

- Four thick carrots
- 2 tbsp avocado oil
- 1 tbsp liquid smoke
- 1/2 tbsp garlic powder
- Salt and pepper to taste

Directions:

1. Preheat the wood pellet grill to 425°F and line a baking sheet with parchment paper.
2. Peel the carrots and round the edges.
3. In a mixing bowl, mix oil, liquid smoke, garlic, salt, and pepper. Place the carrots on the baking dish, then pour the mixture over.
4. Roll the carrots to coat evenly with the mixture and use fingertips to massage the mixture into the carrots.
5. Place in the grill and grill for 35 minutes or until the carrots are fork-tender, ensuring to turn and brush the carrots every 5 minutes with the marinade.
6. Remove from the grill and place the carrots in a hot dog bun. Serve with your favorite toppings and enjoy.

Nutrition:

Calories 149

Total fat 1.6g

Total Carbs 27.9g

Protein 5.4g

Sugar 5.6g

Fiber 3.6g

Sodium: 516mg

Potassium 60mg

CHAPTER 22:

Appetizers and Sides

26. Fresh Creamed Corn

Preparation Time: 5 Minutes

Cooking Time: 30 Minutes

Servings: 4

Ingredients:

- 2 - teaspoons unsalted butter
- 2 - cups fresh corn kernels
- 2 - tablespoons minced shallots
- ¾ - cup 1% low-fat milk
- 2 - teaspoons all-purpose flour
- ¼ - teaspoon salt

Directions:

Melt butter in a huge nonstick skillet over medium-excessive warmness.

Add corn and minced shallots to pan; prepare dinner 1 minute, stirring constantly.

Add milk, flour, and salt to pan; bring to a boil.

Reduce warmness to low; cover and cook dinner 4 minutes.

Nutrition: Calories 107 Fat 3.4g Protein 4g Carb 18g

27. Spinach Salad with Avocado and Orange

Preparation Time: 5 Minutes

Cooking Time: 20 Minutes

Servings: 4

Ingredients:

   1 ½ - tablespoons fresh lime juice

   4 - teaspoons extra-virgin olive oil

   1 - tablespoon chopped fresh cilantro

   1/8 - teaspoon kosher salt

   ½ - cup diced peeled ripe avocado

   ½ - cup fresh orange segments

   1 - (5-ounce) package baby spinach

   1/8 - teaspoon freshly ground black pepper

Directions:

   Combine first 4 substances in a bowl, stirring with a whisk.

   Combine avocado, orange segments, and spinach in a bowl. Add oil combination; toss. Sprinkle salad with black pepper.

Nutrition: Calories 103 Fat 7.3g Sodium 118mg

28. Raspberry and Blue Cheese Salad

Preparation Time: 5 Minutes

Cooking Time: 20 Minutes

Servings: 4

Ingredients:

- 1 ½ - tablespoons olive oil
- 1 ½ - teaspoons red wine vinegar
- ¼ - teaspoon Dijon mustard
- 1/8 - teaspoon salt
- 1/8 - teaspoon pepper
- 5 - cups mixed baby greens
- ½ - cup raspberries
- ¼ - cup chopped toasted pecans
- 1 - ounce blue cheese

Directions:

Join olive oil, vinegar, Dijon mustard, salt, and pepper.

Include blended infant greens; too.

Top with raspberries, walnuts, and blue cheddar.

Nutrition: Calories 133 Fat 12.2g Sodium 193mg

29. Crunchy Zucchini Chips

Preparation Time: 15 Minutes

Cooking Time: 25 Minutes

Servings: 4

Ingredients:

    1/3 - cup whole-wheat panko

    3 - tablespoons uncooked amaranth

    ½ - teaspoon garlic powder

    ¼ - teaspoon kosher salt

    ¼ - teaspoon freshly ground black pepper

    1 - ounce Parmesan cheese, finely grated

    12 - ounces zucchini, cut into

    ¼ - inch-thick slices

    1 - tablespoon olive oil Cooking spray

Directions:

Preheat stove to 425°. Join the initial 6 ingredients in a shallow dish. Join zucchini and oil in an enormous bowl; toss well to coat. Dig zucchini in panko blend, squeezing tenderly to follow. Spot covered cuts on an ovenproof wire rack covered with cooking shower; place the rack on a preparing sheet or jam move dish.

Heat at 425° for 26 minutes or until cooked and fresh. Serve chips right away.

Nutrition: Calories 132 Fat 6.5g Protein 6g Carb 14g Sugars 2g

CHAPTER 23:

Game

30. BBQ Elk Short Ribs

Preparation Time: 10 minutes

Cooking Time: 1 hour

Servings: 6

Ingredients:

1/2-pound green beans

3 pounds' elk short ribs

1/2-pound chanterelle mushrooms

6 ounces' rib rub

Salt as needed

Ground black pepper as needed

4 tablespoons unsalted butter

Direction:

Switch on the Traeger grill, fill the grill hopper with cherry flavored wood pellets, power the grill on by using the control panel, select 'smoke' on the temperature dial, or set the temperature to 275 degrees F and let it preheat for a minimum of 15 minutes.

Meanwhile, prepare the ribs, and for this, season them with salt and rib rub until well coated.

When the grill has preheated, open the lid, place ribs on the grill grate rib-side down, shut the grill and smoke for 30 minutes.

Then wrap ribs in foil in the double layer, return to the grill grate and continue smoking 15 minutes or until the internal temperature reaches 125 degrees.

When done, transfer ribs to a dish and let them rest until required.

Change the smoking temperature to 450 degrees F, shut with lid, and let it preheat for 15 minutes.

Then place a skillet pan on the grill grate and when hot, add butter and when it melts, add mushrooms and beans, toss until mixed, shut with lid, and cook for 15 minutes until vegetables have turned tender and golden brown.

Serve grilled vegetables with elk ribs.

Nutrition:

Calories: 393 Cal

Fat: 16.6 g Carbs: 25 g

Protein: 36 g

Fiber: 0.9 g

CHAPTER 24:

Rubs And Sauces

31. Not-Just-For-Pork Rub

Preparation Time: 5 minutes

Cooking Time: 0 minute

Servings: 4

Ingredients:

- ½ teaspoon ground thyme
- ½ teaspoon paprika
- ½ teaspoon coarse kosher salt
- ½ teaspoon garlic powder
- ½ teaspoon onion powder
- ½ teaspoon chili powder
- ¼ teaspoon dried oregano leaves
- ¼ teaspoon freshly ground black pepper
- ¼ teaspoon ground chipotle chili pepper
- ¼ teaspoon celery seed

Directions:

Using an airtight bag, combine the thyme, paprika, salt, garlic powder, onion powder, chili powder, oregano, black pepper, chipotle pepper, and celery seed. Close the container and shake to mix. Unused rub will keep in an airtight container for months.

Nutrition: Calories: 64 Carbs: 10g Fat: 1g Protein: 1g

32. Chicken Rub

Preparation Time: 5 minutes

Cooking Time: 0 minute

Servings: 4

Ingredients:

2 tablespoons packed light brown sugar

1½ teaspoons coarse kosher salt

1¼ teaspoons garlic powder

½ teaspoon onion powder

½ teaspoon freshly ground black pepper

½ teaspoon ground chipotle chili pepper

½ teaspoon smoked paprika

¼ teaspoon dried oregano leaves

¼ teaspoon mustard powder

¼ teaspoon cayenne pepper

Directions:

Using an airtight bag, combine the brown sugar, salt, garlic powder, onion powder, black pepper, chipotle pepper, paprika, oregano, mustard, and cayenne. Close the container and shake to mix. Unused rub will keep in an airtight container for months.

Nutrition: Calories: 15 Carbs: 3g Fat: 0g Protein: 0g

33. Dill Seafood Rub

Preparation Time: 5 minutes

Cooking Time: 0 minute

Servings: 2

Ingredients:

    2 tablespoons coarse kosher salt

    2 tablespoons dried dill weed

    1 tablespoon garlic powder

    1½ teaspoons lemon pepper

Directions:

Using an airtight bag combine the salt, dill, garlic powder, and lemon pepper. Close the container and shake to mix. Unused rub will keep in an airtight container for months.

Nutrition: Calories: 15 Carbs: 3g Fat: 0g Protein: 0g

34. Cajun Rub

Preparation Time: 5 minutes

Cooking Time: 0 minute

Servings: 2

Ingredients:

    1 teaspoon freshly ground black pepper

    1 teaspoon onion powder

    1 teaspoon coarse kosher salt

    1 teaspoon garlic powder

    1 teaspoon sweet paprika

    ½ teaspoon cayenne pepper

    ½ teaspoon red pepper flakes

    ½ teaspoon dried oregano leaves

    ½ teaspoon dried thyme

    ½ teaspoon smoked paprika

Directions:

Using an airtight bag combine the black pepper, onion powder, salt, garlic powder, sweet paprika, cayenne, red pepper flakes, oregano, thyme, and smoked paprika. Close the container and shake to mix. Unused rub will keep in an airtight container for months.

Nutrition: Calories: 23 Carbs: 2g Fat: 1g Protein: 2g

35. Espresso Brisket Rub

Preparation Time: 5 minutes

Cooking Time: 0 minute

Servings: 2

Ingredients:

- 3 tablespoons coarse kosher salt
- 2 tablespoons ground espresso coffee
- 2 tablespoons freshly ground black pepper
- 1 tablespoon garlic powder
- 1 tablespoon light brown sugar
- 1½ teaspoons dried minced onion
- 1 teaspoon ground cumin

Directions:

Combine the salt, espresso, black pepper, garlic powder, brown sugar, minced onion, and cumin in a small airtight container or zip-top bag,. Close the container and shake to mix. Unused rub will keep in an airtight container for months.

Nutrition: Calories: 56 Carbs: 13g Fat: 1g Protein: 2g

CHAPTER 25:

Snacks

36. Cinnamon Almonds

Preparation Time: 10 Minutes

Cooking Time: 1 Hour and 30 Minutes

Servings: 4 to 6

Ingredients:

    1 egg, the white

    1lb. Almonds

    ½ cup of Brown Sugar

    ½ cup of Granulated sugar

    1/8 tsp. Salt

    1 tbsp. Ground Cinnamon

Directions:

1. Whisk the egg white until frothy. Add the salt, cinnamon, and sugars. Add the almonds and toss to coat.

2. Spread the almonds on a baking dish lined with parchment paper. Make sure they are in a single layer.

3. Preheat the grill to 225F with closed lid.

4. Grill for 1 h and 30 minutes. Stir often.

5. Serve slightly cooled and enjoy!

Nutrition: Calories: 280 Protein: 10g Carbs: 38g Fat: 13g

37. Deviled Eggs

Preparation Time: 15 Minutes

Cooking Time: 30 Minutes

Servings: 4 to 6

Ingredients:

>   3 tsp. Diced chives
>
>   3 tbsp. Mayo
>
>   7 Eggs, hard - boiled, peeled
>
>   1 tsp. Cider vinegar
>
>   1 tsp. Mustard, brown
>
>   1/8 tsp. Hot sauce
>
>   2 tbsp. Crumbled Bacon
>
>   Black pepper and salt to taste
>
>   For dusting: Paprika

Directions:

1. Preheat the grill to 180F with closed lid.

2. Place the cooked eggs on the grate. Smoke 30 minutes. Set aside and let them cool.

3. Slice the eggs in half lengthwise. Scoop the yolks and transfer into a zip lock bag. Now add the black pepper, salt, hot sauce, vinegar, mustard, chives, and mayo.

4. Cut one corner and squeeze the mixture into the egg whites.

5. Top with bacon and dust with paprika.

6. Serve and enjoy! Or chill in the fridge until serving.

Nutrition: Calories: 140 Protein: 6g Carbs: 2g Fat: 6g

Pellet: Hickory

CHAPTER 26:

Smoked Snacks

38. Turkey Jerky

Preparation Time: 30 mins.

Cooking Time: 2 hrs. 30 mins.

Servings: 8

Ingredients:

One T. Asian chili-garlic paste

One T. Curing salt

½ c. Soy sauce

¼ c. Water

Two T. Honey

Two T. Lime juice

Two pounds boneless, skinless turkey breast

Directions:

1.   Mix together the salt, water, lime juice, chili-garlic paste, honey, and soy sauce. Slice the turkey into thin strips. Lay the slices into a large zip-top baggie. If there is more meat that can fit into one bag, use as many as you need. Pour marinade over the turkey. Seal the bag and shake it around so that each slice gets coated with the marinade. Place the bag into the refrigerator overnight. Add wood pellets to your smoker and follow your cooker's startup procedure. Preheat your smoker, with your lid closed, until it reaches 350. Take the sliced turkey out of the bags. Use paper towels to pat them dry. Place them evenly over the grill into one layer. Smoke the turkey for two hours. The jerky should feel dry but still chewable when done. Place into the zip-top bag to keep fresh until ready to eat.

Nutrition: Calories: 80 Protein: 13g Carbs: 5.1g Fat: 0.8g

CHAPTER 27:

Soups And Stews

39. Caldereta Stew

Preparation Time: 30 minutes

Cooking Time: 4 hours

Servings: 12

Ingredients:

- 2lb. Chuck roast, sliced into cubes
- 2tablespoons olive oil
- 1carrot, sliced into cubes
- 2potatoes, sliced into cubes
- 4garlic cloves, chopped
- 2tablespoons tomato paste
- 2cups tomato sauce
- 2red bell peppers, sliced into strips
- 2green bell peppers, sliced into strips
- 2cups of water
- 1/2 cup cheddar cheese, grated
- 1/4 cup liver spread
- Salt to taste

Directions:

Put the beef in a cast iron pan.

Place this in the smoking cabinet.

Open the side dampers and sear slide.

Set the temperature to 375 degrees F.

Smoke the beef for 1 hour and 30 minutes.

Flip the beef and smoke for another 1 hour and 30 minutes.

Add a Dutch oven on top of the grill.

Pour in the olive oil.

Add the carrots and potatoes.

Cook for 5 minutes.

Stir in the garlic and cook for 1 minute.

Transfer the beef to the Dutch oven.

Stir in the tomato paste, tomato sauce, bell peppers, and water.

Bring to a boil.

Reduce temperature to 275 degrees F.

Simmer for 1 hour.

Add the cheese and liver.

Season with the salt.

Nutrition: Calories: 191.1 Fat: 9.3 g Cholesterol: 34 mg Carbohydrates: 15.4 g Fiber: 1.8 g Sugars: 1.3 g Protein: 11.3 g

CHAPTER 28:

Cheese, Nuts, Breads, and Desserts

40. Delicious Donuts on a Grill

Preparation Time: 5 Minutes

Cooking Time: 10 Minutes

Servings: 6

Ingredients:

   1-1/2 cups sugar, powdered

   1/3 cup whole milk

   1/2 teaspoon vanilla extract

   16 ounces of biscuit dough, prepared

   Oil spray, for greasing

   1cup chocolate sprinkles, for sprinkling

Directions:

   Take a medium bowl and mix sugar, milk, and vanilla extract.

   Combine well to create a glaze.

   Set the glaze aside for further use.

   Place the dough onto the flat, clean surface.

   Flat the dough with a rolling pin.

   Use a ring mold, about an inch, and cut the hole in the center of each round dough.

   Place the dough on a plate and refrigerate for 10 minutes.

   Open the grill and install the grill grate inside it.

   Close the hood.

   Now, select the grill from the menu, and set the temperature to medium.

   Set the time to 6 minutes.

Select start and begin preheating.

Remove the dough from the refrigerator and coat it with cooking spray from both sides.

When the unit beeps, the grill is preheated; place the adjustable amount of dough on the grill grate.

Close the hood, and cook for 3 minutes.

After 3 minutes, remove donuts and place the remaining dough inside.

Cook for 3 minutes.

Once all the donuts are ready, sprinkle chocolate sprinkles on top. Enjoy.

Nutrition:

Calories: 400 Total Fat: 11g

Cholesterol: 1mg

Sodium: 787mg

Total Carbohydrate: 71.3g

Dietary Fiber 0.9g

Total Sugars: 45.3g

Protein: 5.7g

41. Bacon Cheese Fries

Preparation time: 10 minutes

Cooking time: 100 minutes

Servings: 2

Ingredients:

 ½-pound bacon slices

 2 large potatoes

 ¼ cup olive oil

 3 teaspoons minced garlic

 ½ teaspoon salt

 ¼ teaspoon ground black pepper

 2 sprigs of rosemary

 ½ cup grated mozzarella cheese

Directions:

Open hopper of the smoker, add dry pallets, make sure ash-can is in place, then open the ash damper, power on the smoker and close the ash damper.

Set the temperature of the smoker to 375 degrees F, let preheat for 30 minutes or until the green light on the dial blinks that indicate smoker has reached to set temperature.

Meanwhile, take a large baking sheet, line it with parchment paper and place bacon slices on it in a single layer.

Place baking sheet on the smoker grill, shut with lid, smoke for 20 minutes, then flip the bacon and continue smoking for 5 minutes or until bacon is crispy.

When done, transfer bacon to a dish lined with paper towels to soak excess fat, then cut bacon into small pieces and set aside until required.

Set the temperature of the smoker to 325 degrees F, let preheat for 15 minutes or until the green light on the dial blinks that indicate smoker has reached to set temperature.

Prepare fries and for this, slice each potato into eight wedges, then spread potato wedges on a rimmed baking sheet in a single layer, drizzle with oil, sprinkle with garlic, salt, black pepper and rosemary and toss until well coat.

Place baking sheet on the smoker grill, shut with lid, smoke for 20 to 30 minutes or until potatoes are nicely golden brown and tender.

Then remove baking sheet from the smoker, sprinkle bacon and cheese on top of fries and continue smoking for 1 minute or until cheese melt.

Serve straight away.

Nutrition: Calories: 388; Total Fat: 22 g; Saturated Fat: 6.8 g; Protein: 9.9 g; Carbs: 38 g; Fiber: 3.5 g; Sugar: 0.5 g

42. Smoked Salted Caramel Apple Pie

Preparation time: 30 mins

Cooking time: 30 mins

Servings: 4 - 6 adult sized humans

Ingredients

For the apple pie:

>   1 pastry (for double crust pie)

>   6 granny smith apples (cored, peeled, and sliced)

For the smoked, salted caramel:

>   1 cup brown sugar

>   ¾ cup light corn syrup

>   6 tablespoons butter (unsalted, cut in pieces)

>   1 cup warm smoked cream

>   1 teaspoon sea salt

Direction:

1.   Grab a large pan and fill it with water and ice.

2.   Grab a shallow, smaller pan, and then put in your cream. Take that smaller pan and place it in the large pan with ice and water.

3.   Set this on your wood pellet smoker grill for 15 to 20 minutes.

4.   For the caramel, mix your corn syrup and sugar in a saucepan, and then cook it all using medium heat. Be sure to stir every so often, until the back of your spoon is coated and begins to turn copper.

5.   Next, add the butter, salt, and smoked cream, and then stir.

6.   Get your pie crust, apples, and salted caramel. Put a pie crust on a pie plate, and then fill it with slices of apples.

7.   Pour on the caramel next.

8.   Put on the top crust over all of that, and then crimp both crusts together to keep them locked in.

9.   Create a few slits in the top crust, so that the steam can be released as you bake.

10.   Brush with some cream or egg, and then sprinkle with some sea salt and raw sugar.

On The Grill

1.   Set up your wood pellet smoker grill for indirect cooking.

2.   Preheat your wood pellet smoker grill for 10 to 15 minutes at 375 degrees Fahrenheit, keeping the lid closed as soon as the fire gets started (should take 4 to 5 minutes, tops).

3.   Set the pie on your grill, and then bake for 20 minutes.

4.   At the 20-minute mark, lower the heat to 325 degrees Fahrenheit, and then let it cook for 35 minutes more. You want the crust to be a nice golden brown, and the filling should be bubbly when it's ready.

5.   Take the pie off the grill, and allow it to cool and rest.

6.   Serve with some vanilla ice cream, and enjoy!

Nutrition: Calories: 552; Total Fat: 19.7 g; Protein: 2.06 g; Carbs: 97.09 g; Fiber: 5.4 g; Sugar: 88.94 g

43. Chocolate Lava Cake with Smoked Whipped Cream

Preparation time: 20 mins

Cooking time: 40 mins

Servings: 4 - 6 adult sized humans

Ingredients

> ½ cup butter
>
> 220 grams semi-sweet chocolate
>
> 1 cup powdered sugar
>
> 2 egg yolks
>
> 2 eggs (large)
>
> 6 tablespoons flour
>
> 1 pint heavy whipping cream
>
> ¼ cup confectioners' sugar
>
> 1 tablespoon bourbon vanilla
>
> 1 tablespoon butter (melted)
>
> Cocoa powder (for dusting)
>
> Confectioners' sugar (for dusting)

Direction:

1. Set up your wood pellet smoker grill for indirect cooking.

2. Start up your wood pellet smoker grill. You just need to get the fire going.

3. Grab an aluminum baking pan, and then add your cream to it.

4. Put the pan on your wood pellet smoker grill, and allow it smoke for 5 minutes.

5. Grab a large mixing bowl, and then pour in your smoked cream. Now keep that in the fridge for later.

6. Turn up your grill to 375 degrees Fahrenheit, and let it preheat, with the lid closed, for 10 to 15 minutes.

7. With 1 tablespoon of butter, brush 4 little souffle cups.

8. Melt your chocolate, as well as what's left of the butter, using a heatproof bowl over boiling water. Stir until it's all smooth and there are no lumps left.

9. Now add your eggs, egg yolks, and powdered sugar, stirring the whole time.

10.   Now, add in the floor whisking it all in, until the whole thing is perfectly blended.

11.   Pour this batter into your souffle cups, then set them on your wood pellet smoker grill and allow them to bake for 13 to 14 minutes — or until the sides are completely set.

12.   Now, take out the smoked cream from your fridge. It should be nice and chilled, at this point.

13.   Add in the bourbon vanilla, and whip it up until it's all airy.

14.   Add in your confectioners' sugar, and don't stop whipping until the cream creates stiff peaks.

15.   Dust some of your lava cakes with cocoa and confectioners' sugar. You may top it all off with a dollop or two of smoky whipped cream.

16.   Serve and enjoy!

Nutrition: Calories: 560; Total Fat: 40.29 g; Protein: 4.63 g; Carbs: 50.15 g; Fiber: 2.2 g; Sugar: 40.18 g

CHAPTER 29:

Desserts

44. Grilled Pound Cake with Fruit Dressing

Preparation Time: 20 min

Cooking Time: 50 min

Servings: 12

Ingredients:

   1 buttermilk pound cake, sliced into 3/4-inch slices

   1/8 cup butter, melted

   1 1/2 cup whipped cream

   1/2 cup blueberries

   1/2 cup raspberries

   1/2 cup strawberries, sliced

Directions:

Preheat pellet grill to 400°F. Turn your smoke setting to high, if applicable.

Brush both sides of each cake slice with melted butter.

Put directly on the grill grate and cook for 5 minutes per side. Turn 90° halfway through cooking each side of the cake for checkered grill marks.

You can cook a couple of minutes longer if you prefer deeper grill marks and smoky flavor.

Remove pound cake slices from the grill and allow it to cool on a plate.

Top slices with whipped cream, blueberries, raspberries, and sliced strawberries as desired. Serve and enjoy!

Nutrition: Calories: 222.1 Fat: 8.7 g Cholesterol: 64.7 mg Carbohydrate: 33.1 g Fiber: 0.4 g Sugar: 20.6 g Protein: 3.4 g

45. Grilled Pineapple with Chocolate Sauce

Preparation Time: 10 min

Cooking Time: 25 min

Servings: 6 to 8

Ingredients:

- 1 pineapple
- 8 oz bittersweet chocolate chips
- 1/2 cup spiced rum
- 1/2 cup whipping cream
- 2 tbsp light brown sugar

Directions:

1. Preheat pellet grill to 400°F.

2. De-skin the pineapple and slice pineapple into 1 in cubes.

3. In a saucepan, combine chocolate chips. When chips begin to melt, add rum to the saucepan. Continue to stir until combined, then add a splash of the pineapple's juice.

4. Add in whipping cream and continue to stir the mixture. Once the sauce is smooth and thickening, lower heat to simmer to keep warm.

5. Thread pineapple cubes onto skewers. Sprinkle skewers with brown sugar.

6. Place skewers on the grill grate.

7. Remove skewers from grill and allow to rest on a plate for about 5 minutes. Serve alongside warm chocolate sauce for dipping.

Nutrition:

Calories: 112.6

Fat: 0.5 g

Cholesterol: 0

Carbohydrate: 28.8 g

Fiber: 1.6 g

Sugar: 0.1 g

Protein: 0.4 g

46. Nectarine and Nutella Sundae

Preparation Time: 10 min

Cooking Time: 25 min

Servings: 4

Ingredients:

- 2 nectarines, halved and pitted
- 2 tsp honey
- 4 tbsp Nutella
- 4 scoops vanilla ice cream
- 1/4 cup pecans, chopped
- Whipped cream, to top
- 4 cherries, to top

Directions:

1. Preheat pellet grill to 400°F.
2. Slice nectarines in half and remove the pits.
3. Brush the inside (cut side) of each nectarine half with honey.
4. Place nectarines directly on the grill grate, cut side down. Cook for 5-6 minutes, or until grill marks develop.
5. Flip nectarines and cook on the other side for about 2 minutes.
6. Remove nectarines from the grill and allow it to cool.
7. Fill the pit cavity on each nectarine half with 1 tbsp Nutella.
8. Place 1 scoop of ice cream on top of Nutella. Top with whipped cream, cherries, and sprinkle chopped pecans. Serve and enjoy!

Nutrition:

Calories: 90

Fat: 3 g

Cholesterol: 0

Carbohydrate: 15g

Fiber: 0

Sugar: 13 g

Protein: 2 g

CHAPTER 30:

Sandwich And Burger

47. BBQ Shredded Beef Burger

Preparation Time: 10 minutes

Cooking Time: 5 hours 10 minutes

Servings: 4

Ingredients

> 3 pounds of boneless chuck roast.
>
> Salt to taste
>
> Pepper to taste
>
> 2 tablespoons of minced garlic
>
> 1 cup of chopped onion
>
> 28 oz. Of barbeque sauce
>
> 6 buns

Directions:

Set the temperature of the Wood Pellet Smoker and Grill to 250 degrees F then preheat for about fifteen minutes with its lid closed. Use a knife to trim off the excess fat present on the roast then place the meat on the preheated grill. Grill the roast for about three and a half hours until it attains an internal temperature of 160 degrees F.

Then, place the chuck roast in an aluminum foil, add in the garlic, onion, barbeque sauce, salt, and pepper then stir to coat. Place the roast bake on the grill and cook for another one and a half hour until an inserted thermometer reads 204 degrees F.

Once cooked, let the meat cool for a few minutes then shred with a fork. Fill the buns with the shredded beef then serve.

Nutrition: Calories 593 Cal Fat 31g Carbohydrates 34g Fiber 1g Protein 44g

48. Grilled Pork Burgers

Preparation Time: 15 minutes

Cooking Time: 1 hour

Servings: 4 – 6

Ingredients

- 1 beaten egg
- 3/4 cup of soft breadcrumbs
- 3/4 cup of grated parmesan cheese
- 1 tablespoon of dried parsley
- 2 teaspoons of dried basil
- 1/2 teaspoon of salt to taste
- 1/2 teaspoon of garlic powder
- 1/4 teaspoon of pepper to taste
- 2 pounds of ground pork
- 6 hamburger buns
- Toppings
- Lettuce leaves
- Sliced tomato
- Sliced sweet onion

Directions:

Add in the egg, bread crumbs, cheese, parsley, basil, garlic powder, salt, and pepper to taste then mix properly to combine. Add in the ground pork then mix properly to combine using clean hands. Form about six patties out the mixture then set aside.

Then, set a Wood Pellet smoker and grill to smoke (250 degrees F) then let it fire up for about five minutes. Place the patties on the grill and smoke for about thirty minutes. Flip the patties over, increase the temperature of the grill to 300 degrees F then grill the patties for a few minutes until an inserted thermometer reads 160 degrees F. Serve the pork burgers on the buns, lettuce, tomato, and onion.

Nutrition: Calories 522 Fat 28g

Carbohydrate 28g Fiber 2g Protein 38g

CHAPTER 31:

Other Recipes

49. Tasty Grilled Pork Chops

Preparation Time: 30 minutes

Cooking Time: 1 hour

Servings: 4

Ingredients:

- 4 pork chops.
- 1/4 cup of olive oil.
- 1 1/2 tablespoons of brown sugar.
- 2 teaspoons of Dijon mustard.
- 1 1/2 tablespoons of soy sauce.
- 1 teaspoon of lemon zest.
- 2 teaspoons of chopped parsley.
- 2 teaspoons of chopped thyme.
- 1/2 teaspoon of salt to taste.
- 1/2 teaspoon of pepper to taste.
- 1 teaspoon of minced garlic.

Directions:

Add in all the ingredients on the list aside from the pork chops then mix properly to combine. This makes the marinade. Place the chops into a Ziploc bag, pour in the prepared marinade then shake properly to coat. Let the pork chops marinate in the refrigerator for about one to eight hours. Then, preheat a Wood Pellet Smoker and Grill to 300 degrees F, place the marinated pork chops on the grill and cook for about six to eight minutes.

Once cooked, let the pork chops rest for about five minutes, slice and serve.

Nutrition: Calories 313, Carbohydrate 5g, Protein 30g, Fat 14g, and Fiber 1g.

50. Delicious Barbeque and Grape Jelly Pork Chops

Preparation Time: 30 minutes

Cooking Time: 1 hour

Servings: 4

Ingredients:

4 boneless pork chops.

1/2 cup of barbeque sauce.

1/4 cup of grape jelly.

2 minced cloves of garlic.

1/2 teaspoon of ground black pepper to taste.

Directions:

Using a small mixing bowl, add in the barbeque sauce, grape jelly, garlic, and pepper to taste then mix properly to combine. Using a resealable plastic bag, add in the pork chops alongside with half of the prepared marinade then shake properly to coat.

Preheat a Wood Pellet Smoker and Grill to 350 degrees F, place the marinated pork chops on the grill, and grill for about six to eight minutes. Flip the pork over, blast with the reserved marinade then grill for an additional six to eight hours until it is cooked through and attains an internal temperature of 145 degrees F.

Once cooked, let the pork rest for about five minutes, slice and serve with your favorite sauce.

Nutrition: Calories 302, Carbohydrates 22g, Protein 29g, Fat 9g, and Fiber 0.8g.

CHAPTER 32:

Measurement Conversions

Volume Equivalents (Liquid)

US STANDARD	US STANDARD (OUNCES)	METRIC (APPROXIMATE)
2 tablespoons	1 fl. Oz.	30 ml
¼ cup	2 fl. Oz.	60 ml
½ cup	4 fl. Oz.	120 ml
1 cup	8 fl. Oz.	240 ml
1½ cups	12 fl. Oz.	355 ml
2 cups or 1 pint	16 fl. Oz.	475 ml
4 cups or 1 quart	32 fl. Oz.	1 L
1 gallon	128 fl. Oz.	4 L

Volume Equivalents (Dry)

US STANDARD	METRIC (APPROXIMATE)
¼ teaspoon	1 ml
½ teaspoon	2 ml
1 teaspoon	5 ml
1 tablespoon	15 ml
¼ cup	59 ml
Cup	79 ml
½ cup	118 ml
1 cup	177 ml

Oven Temperatures

FAHRENHEIT (F)	CELSIUS (C) (APPROXIMATE)
250°F	120 °C
300°F	150°C
325°F	165°C
350°F	180°C
375°F	190°C
400°F	200°C
425°F	220°C
450°F	230°C

Weight Equivalents

US STANDARD	METRIC (APPROXIMATE)
½ ounce	15 g
1 ounce	30 g
2 ounces	60 g
4 ounces	115 g
8 ounces	225 g
12 ounces	340 g
16 ounces or 1 pound	455 g

CHAPTER 33:

Pantry Essentials

Barbecue is defined differently by different people. It's a verb. It's a noun. It's a sauce. It's a type of cooking. It's even considered a flavor of potato chips! When it comes to barbecue recipes, it is often the smoke, temperatures, and cook times that create the secret ingredient. There are only a few pantry must-haves; here's what you'll find in ours.

Allspice: The dried black pimento berry is the key flavor behind jerk seasoning.

Black pepper: For the most vibrant flavor, always grind fresh.

Bouillon cubes: I use these to tuck concentrated umami flavor into tight spaces, like corned beef.

Cajun seasoning

Cayenne pepper

Celery salt and celery seed: The distinct flavor of these spices adds a natural punch of smoke ring-enhancing nitrite. Use them as alternatives to curing salts like Morton Tender Quick. Keep both spices on hand to control the saltiness in your rubs.

Chili powder: The trick to winning a chili cook-off is using the freshest—preferably homemade—chili powder.

Coffee: Great in rubs. I recommend stocking micro-ground instant coffees, such as Starbucks' Via brand.

Coriander (cilantro) seeds: Coriander is the seed of the cilantro plant, but its flavor is not like the cilantro leaf; it tastes a bit like unsweetened Foot Loops cereal. Whole or crushed seeds round out the flavor of robust pork ribs.

Cumin, ground

Garlic, powdered

Ginger, powdered

Mustard, dry

Onions, dried: Dried onions can easily be rehydrated and used for steaming small burgers or as a condiment. They can also add a strong flavor to rubs and marinades.

Paprika, sweet and smoked

Red pepper flakes: A bit goes a long way, but it kicks up the flavor.

Salt, curing: Morton Tender Quick is a venerable brand. Also known as pink salt, Prague powder, or Instar Cure, curing salt will also artificially enhance a smoke ring.

Salt, kosher: Stick to your favorite name brand to control recipe consistency.

Sugar, turbinado: This is also known as raw sugar.

Just A Few Tips About Sugar:

Not all sugar is created equal (no pun intended). Most barbecue smoking rub and sauce recipes call for brown sugar because it adds a deeper flavor to the meat. While you can use regular light or dark brown sugar (which is really just white sugar with added molasses), many pitmasters prefer turbinado sugar (a.k.a. Raw sugar) because its larger crystals add a welcome texture to robust rubs. Bonus: It's less processed and stands up well to heat.

Sugars and sweet sauces are normally added at the very end of high-heat grilling for caramelization, but because you'll typically stick with low-and-slow temperatures when smoking, adding them earlier shouldn't be a problem. Word of caution: Sugar has a scorching point (when it burns) of just above 330°F, so you'll want to watch out for that when using your wood pellet grill's higher heat settings.

Sauce It Up!

Mustard: In smoking prep, you can use mustard as a no-fuss adherent for rubs. Keep it simple and stick with cheap yellow table mustard, unless otherwise directed in a recipe. It's also the base for South Carolina-style sauces.

Vinegar: Apple cider vinegar provides a tart punch to a sauce recipe. It plays a starring role in North Carolina–style barbecue sauces.

Worcestershire sauce: Only use high-quality brands, because the punch behind its flavor comes from anchovies; generics often skip the fish.

CHAPTER 34:

Cookout Tips

With proper planning and plenty of time, you can consolidate a menu and cook several recipes at once. Here are some tips to maximize your pellet-powered cookout:

Orchestrate a detailed timeline for your smoking day. This should culminate with the reveal of your centerpiece meat as your friends and family are just getting settled in. Don't forget to account for the meat's resting time.

Serve it hot. Take care with the resting process and be sure you still serve your dish hot. Hot food pulls in more senses like smell. For example, nothing is better than hot pizza—even cheap pizza! That steaming slice on the ride home is as good as it gets. Hot food gets people's attention on a primal level.

Use secondary grill shelves as a staging area for appetizers with shorter cook times. Quick-cooking veggies can be added last and will hold until serving.

Avoid peeking and allow for extra cook time when adding cold food alongside items already cooking in the pellet grill.

Allow for good smoke flow across your entire grate surface. Avoid crowding the food, and leave 1 to 2 inches of space surrounding food pieces.

Because wood pellet grill smokers offer high temperatures in addition to low, you can make some things quickly or in advance, such as appetizers, smoked nuts and cheeses, and desserts. Of course, when cooking for a really large crowd, it might help if you cook or finish a couple of side dishes in the oven or have a neighbor bring over an extra grill.

CHAPTER 35:

A Few Final Tips

Sweet finish: Hold sweet sauces until the end of your cook because sugar burns quickly. Consider cutting out the sugar or just serving sauce as an optional side. There's an old saying, "Taste the flavor in the meat when the sauce is on the side."

Back to the grind: Eliminate boring black pepper shakers. Grinding your own fresh whole black peppercorns will add next-level flavor, guaranteed.

Convection: The convection oven–like qualities of your pellet grill are unique in the barbecue world. The even heat and circulation may reduce cook times for recipes designed for other types of smokers.

Tongs, not forks: You don't want to pierce, puncture, or prick the exterior surface of your barbecue, especially sausage and poultry, because that will drain out those fabulous and flavorful juices from the meat. Use that long barbecue fork for a tent spike instead. Seriously, jam it into the ground and use it to secure your tailgating tent! Just don't use it on meat and drain those flavorful juices if you don't have to.

Fire safety: Have a dedicated fire extinguisher on hand that is rated for grease fires as well as wood, and be ready to use it. Most competitions require you to have one at your cook site, and they're not expensive.

Shut it down: Remember to shut down your pellet grill using Traeger's recommended process. This method will burn out excess pellets so your grill's firepot is empty and safely ready for the next cook.

Conclusion

With the help of this Wood Pellet Smoker and Grill cookbook, you will be able to elevate your grilling skills and to learn how to be a master in grilling in no time; and with simple instructions and easy-to-follow recipes. So, if you have tried hard to grill and you failed before; this cookbook will show you the right way to do it.

You will learn that grilling is a true skill that can be learned and you

You will be surprised at how easy it is to use grilling meat at a low temperature for a long period of time. Learn right now that all it takes to learn to grill is to have a Wood Pellet Smoker and Grill and start without fear of burning foods. Included in this book; you will find a large variety of affordable ingredients starting from meats; seafood ingredients, poultry, and even vegetables. With this cookbook, you will end up enjoying a heaven of recipes. And what is more enjoyable about this book is that you won't need any special equipment; all you have to do is to gather a few affordable ingredients and the results will be mesmerizing and beyond your imagination.

So are you ready to make a change in your life and to change your cooking rituals once and forever; if your answer is yes; then get ready because you are about to read one of the best cookbooks you can ever find and stumble into. Make sure to buy the Wood Pellet Smoker and Grill Recipe cookbook to start your cooking journey.

There are numerous ways to achieve a smoky flavor in your food. However, if there is one that stands out from its counterparts, then it is the Wood Pellet Smoker-Grill. While you may prefer the older versions simply because you know how they work, you may want to consider the technologically advanced version, as it is undoubtedly a one-stop smoker solution.

Further, you can experiment with the wood pellets, thereby enhancing your cooking experience. What's more, you can pack flavor into your meals as you spend lesser time slogging over your favorite recipes. All the recipes include the cooking time and calorie counts to help you plan. There are various recipes for people trying to watch their diets and eat a low-calorie meal. Just try these mouth-smacking recipes and happy cooking!

Printed by BoD™in Norderstedt, Germany